Let's Get Healthy, Saints!

THE GUIDE FOR BIBLICAL HEALTH

DOMINIQUE BIERMAN, PHD

Published by Zion's Gospel Press
52 Tuscan Way, Ste 202-412
St. Augustine, FL, 32092
shalom@ZionsGospel.com

Paperback ISBN: 978-1-953502-39-1
E-Book ISBN: 978-1-953502-40-7

On occasion words such as Jesus, Christ, Lord, and God have been changed by the author, back to their original Hebrew renderings, Yeshua, Messiah, Yahveh, and Elohim.

Bold or italicized emphasis or underlining within quotations is the author's own.

Printed in the United States of America
First Printing 1991, Second Printing August 2021, Third Printing August 2023

ZIONS GOSPEL
PRESS

PREAMBLE

In the year 1991, my first edition of *Let's Get Healthy, Saints!** was printed.

This book was based on the inspiration of the Holy Spirit coupled with my experience as a nutritionist, health consultant, and health food store owner in Israel. I used the Bible as the major foundation for the book. It was very well received and blessed many people with godly and commonsense principles on how to lead a healthy lifestyle and prevent disease.

However, over the years, my ministry became quite involved and my schedule hectic – and, after many moves and many trips into many nations, I lost the manuscript! I cannot think of a better time to rewrite the book with even more information and by the power of His Spirit. The lead Scripture was then and still is the following:

> The thief comes only to steal, slaughter, and destroy. I have come that they might have life and have it abundantly!
>
> John 10:10

The main principle of this book is simple: Whatever steals, kills, and destroys in our lifestyle is from Satan and whatever brings an abundance of health and wellbeing is of Yah (God).

For abundance of life! Lechayim!
Archbishop Dr. Dominiquae Bierman

*   **Disclaimer:** The information in this book is for your personal consideration. I am not a medical doctor. If you need medical advise please contact your health care provider.

CONTENTS

CHAPTER ONE

The Mother of All Sins: Lust

> For all that is in the world—the lust and sensual craving of the flesh and the lust and longing of the eyes and the boastful pride of life [pretentious confidence in one's resources or in the stability of earthly things]—these do not come from the Father, but are from the world.
>
> **1 John 2:16 AMP**

DEFINITION OF LUST: Intense sexual desire or appetite; uncontrolled or illicit sexual desire or appetite; lecherousness; a passionate or overmastering desire or craving (usually followed by) a lust for power. (From Dictionary.com)

Most of the modern-day diseases can be prevented with the right nutrition, both spiritual and physical.

From the start, breaking the nutritional laws of the Creator caused disastrous results. Adam and his wife had all the fruit trees in the Garden of Eden at their disposal, but they craved the only fruit Elohim forbade them to have.

> **And the Lord God commanded the man, saying, "You may freely (unconditionally) eat [the fruit] from every tree of the garden; but [only] from**

> the tree of the knowledge (recognition) of good
> and evil you shall not eat, otherwise on the day
> that you eat from it, you shall most certainly die
> [because of your disobedience]."
>
> Genesis 2:16-17 AMP

Then the snake, possessed with the spirit and nature of Satan, lied, perverted truth, and tempted the woman. It enticed the woman to follow the strong desire she had for the forbidden fruit. The snake used *lust* to tempt the woman.

> Now the woman saw that the tree was good for
> food, and that it was a thing of lust for the eyes,
> and that the tree was desirable for imparting
> wisdom. So she took of its fruit and she ate. She
> also gave to her husband who was with her and
> he ate.
>
> Genesis 3:6

Upon their eating of the forbidden tree, they became mentally sick right away! They were now plagued with fear and guilt, and they hid from the presence of their loving Creator.

> But the LORD God called to Adam, and said
> to him, "Where are you?" He said, "I heard the
> sound of You [walking] in the garden, and I was
> afraid because I was naked; so I hid myself."
>
> Genesis 3:9-10 AMP

Then the blame-shifting began. The man blamed the woman - the woman blamed the snake - and basically, they all blamed God for creating the other one.

We need to settle it once and for all: Disease is always connected with our spiritual and mental condition. Once they broke Elohim's Commandment, they became spiritually and mentally sick; physical disease would then follow.

Physical disease is never the root cause: it is rather the outcome of the separation from the Creator due to disobedience. Nowadays, doctors are treating physical bodies apart from spiritual and emotional conditions. That is the reason people are addicted to their doctors and to many harmful medications but never get healthy. Most of humanity has forsaken the doctor of doctors, *YHVH Rophe*, and His manual of instruction for health and wellbeing - namely the Torah and the whole Bible.

> He taught me and said to me, "Let your heart hold fast my words; keep my Commandments and live."
>
> Hear, my son, and accept my sayings, and the years of your life will be many.
>
> My son, pay attention to my words and be willing to learn; open your ears to my sayings. Do not let them escape from your sight; keep them in the center of your heart. For they are life to those who find them, and healing and health to all their flesh.
>
> Proverbs 4:4, 10, 20-22 AMP

His Word is healing to all our flesh because of two major reasons:

His Word instructs us how to live holy and healthy lives.

His Word has creative power of its own, as Elohim created everything by His Word.

It gathers then that if we follow His instructions, together with meditating and proclaiming His Word, we will be healthy and whole. It's that simple!

> This Book of the Law (Torah) shall not depart from your mouth, but you shall read [and meditate on] it day and night, so that you may be careful to do [everything] in accordance with all that is written in it; for then you will make your way prosperous, and then you will be successful.
>
> Joshua 1:8 AMP

> Death and life are in the power of the tongue, and those who love it and indulge it will eat its fruit and bear the consequences of their words.
>
> Proverbs 18:21 AMP

We literally do "eat our words." If our words are contrary to His words and they are full of the poison of unbelief and skepticism, we will be sick in spirit, soul, and body.

But if our words align with His Words, they have creative miracle power to bring healing, wholeness, and breakthrough.

> For as the rain and snow come down from Heaven, and do not return there without having watered the earth, making it bring forth and sprout, giving seed to sow and bread to eat, so

My word will be that goes out from My mouth. It will not return to Me in vain, but will accomplish what I intend, and will succeed in what I sent it for.

Isaiah 55:10-11 TLV

Shut your ears to the lies of the snake. Repent of all lust. Keep His commandments for your life and align your words with His Words!

He said, "If you diligently listen to the voice of (YHVH) Adonai, your God, do what is right in His eyes, pay attention to His mitzvot (Commandments), and keep all His decrees, I will put none of the diseases on you which I have put on the Egyptians. For I am Adonai who heals you."

Exodus 15:26

PRAYER

Father, forgive me for listening to the lies of the snake, tempting me to indulge in food lust, sexual lust, and money lust. I repent of lust and surrender my life to You, Yeshua Messiah. Come and fill me with Your Holy Spirit and write Your commandments in my heart and mind. I choose both my spiritual and physical diet to be directed by Your Word and principles. Amen.

CHAPTER TWO

Bad Genes

Do not bow down to them or worship them. For
I, (YHVH) Adonai, your God, am a jealous God,
visiting the iniquity of the fathers on the children
and on the third and fourth generation of those
who hate Me, but showing lovingkindness to a
thousand generations of those who love Me and
keep My mitzvot.

                                        Deuteronomy 5:9-10

DISEASE CAN BE inherited genetically, and this will be
called a family curse. Doctors call it "bad genes" when
they see a certain disease reoccurring in a family. The Holy
Scriptures are clear about this and in many places, it talks
about "visiting" or suffering for the sins or iniquities of our ancestors. This suffering can take many shapes, like reoccurring
accidents, failures, tragedies, divorces, family violence, gender
confusion, bankruptcies, poverty, addictions, as well as mental
and physical diseases.

You shall not have other gods beside Me. Do
not make for yourself a graven image—no image
of what is in the heavens above or on the earth

> beneath or in the water under the earth. Do not bow down to them or worship them. For I, (YHVH) Adonai your God, am a jealous God, visiting the iniquity of the fathers on the children and on the third and fourth generation of those who hate Me, but showing lovingkindness to a thousand generations of those who love Me and keep My mitzvot.
>
> Deuteronomy 5:7-10

The main reason for these family curses or "bad genes" is idolatry, which includes witchcraft, occultic and cultic practices, ancestral worship, new age practices, channeling spirit guides, Freemasonry, secret societies (including some fraternities/sororities), the use of "drug trips", celebrating pagan feasts, sexual immorality, homosexuality, harboring pagan traditions, spilling of innocent blood like abortions and murder, and more.

Another form of idolatry that brings a family curse is trusting in man above God. The humanism of the 21st century that puts man in the center has this society very sick, both mentally and physically.

> Thus says (YHVH) Adonai: "Cursed is the one who trusts in man, and depends on flesh as his arm, and whose heart turns from (YHVH) ADONAI. For he will be like a bush in the desert. He cannot see goodness when it comes, but will dwell in parched places in the wilderness— a salt land where no one lives."
>
> Jeremiah 17:5-6

Another important factor in family curses is repaying good for evil:

Whoever rewards evil for good— evil will never leave his house.

Proverbs 17:13

For example, many people are under a curse for dishonoring and disrespecting Israel and the Jewish People. *YHVH* used His chosen people to bring the Bible to all mankind. He also used a Jewish virgin to birth a Jewish Messiah that would save the whole world.

Therefore, whoever dishonors, disrespects, or does evil to Israel and the Jews would be under a serious family curse.

My desire is to bless those who bless you, but whoever curses you I will curse, and in you all the families of the earth will be blessed.

Genesis 12:3

These family curses can reoccur until the third, the fourth, and even the tenth generation, especially those that concern the nation's relationship with Israel.

No one born of forbidden relations (outside of holy matrimony) is to enter the community of (YHVH) Adonai —even to the tenth generation, none of his descendants are to enter the community of (YHVH) Adonai. No Ammonite or Moabite is to enter the community of (YHVH) Adonai —even to the tenth generation none

> belonging to them is to enter the community of
> (YHVH) Adonai forever— because they did not
> meet you (Israel) with bread and water on the
> way when you came out from Egypt, and because
> they hired against you Balaam son of Beor from
> Petor of Aram-naharaim to curse you.
>
> Deuteronomy 23:3-5

Since these family curses also manifest in the form of mental and physical disease, what can be done? Are we to be under these curses and diseases all the days of our lives?

Here's the best news you will hear: You can be free from all family curses when you repent for your sins and those of your ancestors and surrender your life to serve the living God through Messiah Yeshua!

> The Messiah redeemed us from the curse
> pronounced in the Torah by becoming cursed
> on our behalf; for the Tanakh (Hebrew Holy
> Scriptures) says, "Everyone who hangs from a
> stake comes under a curse." Yeshua the Messiah
> did this so that in union with him the Gentiles
> might receive the blessing announced to
> Avraham, so that through trusting and being
> faithful, we might receive what was promised,
> namely, the Spirit.
>
> Galatians 3:13-14 CJB

> So was fulfilled what was spoken through Isaiah
> the prophet, saying, "He Himself took our

sicknesses and carried away our diseases."

Matthew 8:17

PRAYER

Heavenly Father, I hereby repent and forsake all my sins and the sins of my ancestors in the areas of idolatry, sexual immorality, humanism, and anti-Semitism. I ask You to forgive me and break all these family curses and diseases from me, for the sake of Your Son, my Jewish Messiah Yeshua, who took all my curses and diseases upon Himself on the execution tree in Golgotha. Amen.

CHAPTER THREE

Root Causes of Disease #1
The Love of Money

> Even so, every good tree produces good fruit,
> but the rotten tree produces bad fruit. A good
> tree cannot produce bad fruit, nor can a rotten
> tree produce good fruit.
>
> Matthew 7:17-18

EVERYTHING IN LIFE is connected with sowing and reaping, root and fruit. Whatever we sow, we reap. If we sow tomatoes, we will reap tomatoes - we cannot expect to reap dates or olives instead. The attitudes of our life, our thoughts, words, and deeds are like seeds that when sown will eventually bring forth a harvest. In the last chapter we talked about bad genes or generational curses, which dealt with the sowing of "bad seeds" in our ancestors. But in this chapter, we will deal with our own bad sowing and its consequences. Then we will learn to sow right and reap a harvest of righteousness and health.

There are three devastating root causes of disease and early death:

1. The love of money
2. Jealousy
3. Bitterness

THE LOVE OF MONEY

> For the love of money is the root of all kinds of evil—some, longing for it, have gone astray from the faith and pierced themselves through with many sorrows.
>
> 1 Timothy 6:10

This is a type of idolatry harbored by the rich and the poor alike. When we consider money as a determining factor for our obedience to *YHVH*, it is an idol. I cannot count the numerous times that I have heard this false statement: "I cannot tithe because I earn very little" or "I cannot obey what Yah (God) showed me to do because I do not have the money." We need to settle it once and for all: Obedience to the Almighty does not depend on what you have in your pocket. It depends on faith and our humility to walk in faith only.

> **(YHVH) Adonai is my shepherd; I shall not want.**
>
> Psalm 23:1

When Rabbi Baruch, my husband, and I were sent to the nations from Jerusalem in 1990, we had no money and not even suitcases. We landed in the USA with a few bundles and a heart full of faith. Then the Holy Spirit began to lead us from there, and over thirty years later, we have traveled to more than fifty nations, hundreds of cities and have ministered salvation, deliverance, healing, and restoration to many thousands of people. I have written and published about twenty books, thousands of articles, TV programs, music albums and

Shabbat letters, and I lead two non-profit organizations and an international global team.

We started from zero, with only faith and obedience. We never gave an excuse to YHVH that we could not travel somewhere because of no money. Sometimes we were packed and ready to go on the way to the airport before the money came in a miraculous way. Sometimes we worked a regular job together with full-time ministry so we would have funds to give and to go. We have tithed from the top when we had little and when we had much. We sought to sow in faith, and YHVH has always met us.

> The point is this: Whoever sows sparingly shall also reap sparingly, and whoever sows bountifully shall also reap bountifully. Let each one give as he has decided in his heart, not grudgingly or under compulsion—for God loves a cheerful giver. And God is able to make all grace overflow to you, so that by always having enough of everything, you may overflow in every good work.
>
> 2 Corinthians 9:6-8

I have been a mother to two wonderful special needs children, and their treatments and needs demanded much money, which I did not personally have, being a traveling minister for so many years. But my Father in Heaven sent me a wonderful Israeli woman, a benefactress who was not even a believer in Messiah, to cover most of the very expensive treatments and financial needs of my children. I did not leave the ministry and what I knew to be the will of Yah to instead go and make money - He provided miraculously for the needs of my children.

Then my sowing into the nations began to bear fruit, and many of our disciples began to bless us financially, and we could contribute more and more to the special needs of all our children. Even when we had nothing, we never lacked! We always felt like millionaires inside because we serve the richest Father in the Universe. And we are givers because He is a giver! Stinginess leads to disease; generosity makes us whole!

> **The generous man will be prosperous, and he who waters will himself be watered.**
>
>

Proverbs 11:25 NASB
>

But most people put money above obedience, and they get old and sick because they worship money instead of the One who is our Shepherd and Provider. His desire is for us to be prosperous, but not to worship prosperity – we must worship Him alone! Being generous towards Him and others causes our souls to prosper.

> **Beloved, I pray that in all respects you may prosper and be in good health, just as your soul prospers.**
>
>

3 John 2 NASB
>

We sowed our lives, breath, and time and the little we had into the Kingdom. And we are now, thirty years later, reaping the benefit of these good seeds that have brought us prosperity and health. The word is *Shalom*, which is wellbeing in general or wholeness, where nothing is missing, broken, or lacking.

When you put money or the lack of it in the center of your life - excusing yourself from following Him all the way because of the lack of it or because of the abundance of it - you will be piercing yourself with many sorrows. The first disease that you will suffer will be in your soul, where sorrow is going to reside, bringing depression and emotional problems because of the idolatry of money. Then the emotional disease will develop into physical infirmities, including terminal ones. Having money or the lack thereof as your god is a very dangerous thing: it is rooted in unbelief, self-centeredness, and greed.

There was a rich young ruler that Yeshua invited to become part of His disciples, but he refused because it entailed trusting the Messiah rather than his possessions. He could have been the 12th apostle after Judas betrayed the Master and killed himself. But this rich young man preferred his possessions and from then on became depressed.

> *Yeshua* said to him, "If you wish to be perfect, go, sell what you own, and give to the poor; and you will have treasure in Heaven. Then come, follow Me." But when the young man heard this statement, he went away grieving, for he had much property.
> Matthew 19:21-22

Can you imagine? He chose his money over Yeshua's calling, and from then on, he *grieved*, because he had grieved the Holy Spirit with this bad choice rooted in the worship of money. He may have been depressed and grieved all his life thereafter and probably could not even enjoy his possessions.

YHVH wants us to prosper and to succeed in all He called us to do on earth, even to enjoy our lives, as long as He remains the center of our being. When He is the one blessing and prospering us, there is no grief or sorrow involved. Below is one of my favorite Scriptures about this (using many translations to convey the truth from the Hebrew in it):

> The Birkat Hashem, it maketh wealthy, and He addeth no sorrow with it.
>
> Proverbs 10:22 OJB

> The good that comes from the Lord makes one rich, and He adds no sorrow to it.
>
> Proverbs 10:22 NLV

> The blessing of (YHVH) *ADONAI* brings wealth and He adds no trouble with it.
>
> Proverbs 10:22

The Blessing of YHVH is majorly an outcome of obedience coupled with faithful hard work. You must be faithful in whatever you are called to do if you are to prosper. If you work a job to provide for your family or if you are in full-time ministry or both, faithfulness is the Kingdom Principle, not greed or stinginess or running after money which will pierce you with many sorrows. We must be faithful to invest the gifts, talents, and opportunities that He gives us.

> His Master said to him, 'Well done, good and faithful servant! You were faithful with a little, so I'll put you in charge of much. Enter into your Master's joy!'
>
> Matthew 25:23

> For to the one who has, more shall be given, and
> he shall have an abundance. But from the one
> who does not have, even what he does have shall
> be taken away.
>
> Matthew 25:29

Being obedient, faithful, and hard-working is good for the soul and therefore also good for the body, for a healthy body, and a healthy soul go hand in hand.

> Lazy hands make a man poor, but diligent hands
> bring wealth.
>
> Proverbs 10:4

> The hand of the diligent will rule, but the lazy
> will become forced labor.
>
> Proverbs 12:24

One of my favorite Scriptures is about how righteous giving delivers from early and sudden death:

> Riches make no profit in the day of wrath, but
> righteousness delivers from death.
>
> Proverbs 11:4

In Hebrew, the word *righteousness* is *Zedaka*, which also means "to give alms or to give righteously." This is a typical example of how when we give according to His will and principles, we have supernatural protection over our health and lives.

To sum it all up, the way you relate to money will determine your wellbeing. If you put Yah in the center and are faithful to work hard wherever He puts you, and give generously, you will prosper in soul, body, and finances. If you are lazy, stingy, and worship money or give Him money excuses of why you can't obey Him, you will be grieved and sick in your soul. Your quality of life will be poor, and your mental and physical health will suffer.

> No one can serve two masters; for either he will hate the one and love the other, or he will stick by one and look down on the other. You cannot serve God and money.
>
> Matthew 6:24

Overcoming Worry with Trust (Worry Brings Disease!)

> So I say to you, do not worry about your life— what you will eat or drink, or about your body, what you will wear. Isn't life more than food and the body more than clothing?
>
> Look at the birds of the air. They do not sow or reap or gather into barns; yet your Father in Heaven feeds them. Are you not of more value than they? And which of you by worrying can add a single hour to his life? And why do you worry about clothing? Consider the lilies of the field, how they grow. They neither toil nor spin. Yet I tell you that not even Solomon in all his glory

clothed himself like one of these. Now if in this way God clothes the grass—which is here today and thrown into the furnace tomorrow—will He not much more clothe you, O you of little faith?

Therefore do not worry, saying, 'What will we eat?' or 'What will we drink?' or 'What will we wear?' For the pagans eagerly pursue all these things; yet your Father in Heaven knows that you need all these. But seek first the Kingdom of God and His righteousness, and all these things shall be added to you. Therefore do not worry about tomorrow, for tomorrow will worry about itself. Each day has enough trouble of its own.

Matthew 6:25-34

PRAYER

Heavenly Father, forgive me for putting money, possessions, or my desire for them above You, Your will and Your Word for my life. I have been worried and have pierced myself with many sorrows. I repent in dust and ashes, and I make You the Elohim of my life and finances. I place my trust in You as I apply myself to be faithful to work and/or to minister and to do all You have appointed me to do. I ask your forgiveness for withholding obedience, tithes, and offerings from You and from my pastors and mentors and from putting my affairs above the affairs of Your

Kingdom. From now on, everything that I have, own, or even desire is surrendered to You, to Your will and to Your ways forever. I will be faithful with little and with much, without excuses. In Yeshua's name. Amen.

CHAPTER FOUR

Root Causes of Disease #2 Jealousy & Envy

> Even so, every good tree produces good fruit, but the rotten tree produces bad fruit. A good tree cannot produce bad fruit, nor can a rotten tree produce good fruit.
>
> Matthew 7:17-18 TLV

JEALOUSY IS ONE of the major traits of Satan. He has been jealous of mankind from the start. Satan is a fallen angel; as important as angels are, they are not the crown of Elohim's creation - man is.

> How you have fallen from Heaven, O brightstar, son of the dawn! How you are cut down to the earth, you who made the nations prostrate! You said in your heart: "I will ascend to Heaven, I will exalt my throne above the stars of God. I will sit upon the mount of meeting, in the uttermost parts of the north. I will ascend above the high places of the clouds—I will make myself like Elyon." Yet you will be brought down to Sheol,

to the lowest parts of the Pit.

Isaiah 14:12-15

So, from the beginning, he has been mentally sick with jealousy and hatred against mankind, especially against the Jewish people from whom the last Adam, the Messiah, would come to rule Israel and the nations. This jealousy is the root cause of all anti-Semitism.

Among some of the Christians and the Arabs, black and white, there is jealousy against the Jews for being the Chosen People of YHVH forever. This jealousy has led to horrible crimes, murder, and torture of Jews for thousands of years. It is the root cause of the Christian Crusades, the Spanish Inquisition, and the Holocaust. It is also the root cause of all the wars against Israel in the Middle East. Ishmael and Esau have been jealous of Isaac and Jacob. This is an ancient hatred rooted in jealousy.[1]

> **Wrath is cruel, and anger is overwhelming, but who can stand before jealousy?**
>
> **Proverbs 27:4**

> **Because of your violence to your brother Jacob, shame will cover you, and you will be cut off forever.**
>
> **Obadiah 1:10**

Jealousy is devastating, and it leads to murder, like when Cain murdered Abel because God chose Abel's offering but rejected Cain's.

---

[1]   Read my book *The Identity Theft* at www.against-antisemitism.com

Then He said, "What have you done? The voice of your brother's blood is crying out to Me from the ground. So now, cursed are you from the ground which opened its mouth to receive your brother's blood from your hand. As often as you work the ground, it will not yield its crops to you again. You will be a restless wanderer on the earth."

Genesis 4:10-12

The result of a jealous or envious life is the curse of restlessness; this, in turn, brings about many mental and physical diseases. When people are restless, it secretes chemical substances in the body that affect blood pressure and sugar levels. Jealousy is always coupled with anger, and so your body and soul become toxic. In fact, jealousy causes your entire skeletal system of bones to crumble from within. ADHD (Attention Deficit Hyperactive Disorder) might be connected with the root of jealousy among siblings, especially due to feelings of rejection from one or both parents.

A tranquil heart is life to the body, but envy is rottenness to the bones.

Proverbs 14:30

When the bones rot, people can have minor falls and break bones, hips, and everything right and left. On top of this, because the immune system is in the bone marrow, if the bones are not healthy, then the immune system will be impaired and unable to adequately deal with disease and infections. I cannot think of a better spiritual vaccine against infections and viruses than repentance from jealousy. Restoring our minds to contentedness without envy immunizes us from mental and physical disease. Being humble and magnanimous with others, enjoying and applauding their successes, will go a long way toward making us whole in our bones and in our immune system.

Do not covet what others have or their positions or possessions. Be faithful to cultivate the life and garden that you have been given and to celebrate other people's successes.

> **Keep your lifestyle free from the love of money, and be content with what you have. For God Himself has said, "I will never leave you or forsake you,"**
>
> **Hebrews 13:5**

> **Do not covet your neighbor's house, your neighbor's wife, his manservant, his maidservant, his ox, his donkey, or anything that is your neighbor's.**
>
> **Exodus 20:17**

Envy, jealousy, or covetousness has its source in demonic wisdom. These attitudes make people sick, perverted in spirit, soul, and body. They are very dangerous!

> **Who among you is wise and understanding? By his good conduct let him show his deeds in the gentleness of wisdom. But if you have bitter jealousy and selfish ambition in your heart, do**

not boast and lie against the truth. This is not the wisdom that comes down from above, but is earthly, unspiritual, demonic. For where jealousy and selfish ambition exist, there is disorder and every evil practice. But the wisdom that is from above is first pure, then peaceable, gentle, open to reason, full of mercy and good fruits, impartial, not hypocritical. And the fruit of righteousness is sown in shalom by those who make shalom.

Yakov (James) 3:13-18

Cultivate the wisdom from above, and you will be sowing seeds of Shalom and will reap Shalom, which means wholeness, peace, joy, health, wellbeing, prosperity, completeness.

Prayer

Father in Heaven, I confess having jealousy in my heart. I have allowed this wicked trait of Satan to plague my thoughts and attitudes. I ask Your forgiveness and break any covenant with jealousy and even any kind of antisemitism in Yeshua's name. Thank You for forgiving me and cleansing me from all unrighteousness all the way to my bones, bone marrow and immune system. Amen.

CHAPTER FIVE

Root Causes of Disease #3 Unforgiveness & Bitterness

Even so, every good tree produces good fruit,
but the rotten tree produces bad fruit. A good
tree cannot produce bad fruit, nor can a rotten
tree produce good fruit.

Matthew 7:17-18

MANY PEOPLE ARE sick and defiled because of unforgiveness and bitterness. Bitterness in the heart is like a festering wound, full of puss and toxic waste that can never heal. This is killing people with depression, schizophrenia, and a myriad of mental sicknesses, in addition to cancer, arthritis, and all kinds of physical sicknesses. But above all that, unforgiveness puts us under the judgment of Yah (God) and breaks down our relationship with the Holy Spirit and with others.

See to it that no one falls short of the grace of
God; and see to it that no bitter root springs up
and causes trouble, and by it many be defiled.

Hebrews 12:15

When bitterness is in our hearts, there will be no grace; when there is no grace, there is no healing and no wholeness. Forgiveness is one of the major keys to healing. But forgiveness is not agreement with the crimes and sins committed against us. It is not denial or sanctioning the abuses and the offenses. It is acknowledging them and the pain that we have suffered and, just like Yeshua did on the cross, letting them go and getting ourselves free from their toxic effects. Forgiveness and release from our judgment is an act of our will in obedience to the One who forgave the unforgivable!

I have lived this message throughout more than thirty-two years of service to the God of Israel through Yeshua the Messiah. I cannot think of anything more powerful in the world than forgiveness. No atomic bombs, no H bombs, no dynamite, no power on earth can compare with the simple fact that only forgiveness has the ability to change your life and to change the world.

> **For if you forgive others their transgressions, your heavenly Father will also forgive you. But if you do not forgive others, neither will your Father forgive your transgressions.**
> **Matthew 6:14-15**

Yeshua made that decision on the cross while being executed by the Roman Empire and a group of Jews hired by the apostate high priest who were crying "crucify Him." He said this while bleeding and in excruciating pain and humiliation, naked and extremely wounded:

"Father forgive them for they do not know what they are doing."[2]

This declaration is resounding through the ages. It is the power of this forgiveness that can change a world full of violence and hatred. Jews and Gentiles were absolved that day by the Jewish Messiah, the Master of the Universe! Whoever would come to Him in repentance for their sins would obtain that forgiveness.

> **Therefore He is also able to save completely those who draw near to God through Him, always living to make intercession for them.**
>
> **Hebrews 7:25**

While visiting Toledo, the seat of the Spanish Inquisition in Spain in the 1490s, I used the power of forgiveness in the Catholic Church of Santa Maria La Blanca. Yah sent me there and supernaturally revealed to me that this had been the major synagogue in the past. In 1492, all Jews that refused to convert to Christianity were expelled from Spain (and later from Portugal), my Sephardic Jewish ancestors included. This synagogue had been confiscated and converted into a church before the expulsion.

It was there that I released forgiveness over Spain and all Christians. As a descendant of the humiliated, tortured, spoiled, and expelled Jews, I have the power to forgive. Not to sanction, but yes to forgive; not to forget, but yes to forgive.

I hugged the nun in charge, who was very puzzled about my prayers inside the church. She witnessed that I was on the floor (decorated with Rosetta-type stars of David, reminiscent

---

[2]   Luke 23:32

of the Jewish past of the church) weeping, praying, repenting, and mourning for the terrible massacre, the *auto-da-fé*,[3] the flames of the Inquisition. When the nun at the exit asked me with a stern demeanor what I was doing, I answered: "I am a Sephardic (Spanish) Jew, and your people humiliated, robbed, killed, and expelled my family. But because Yeshua, the Jewish Messiah, whom you call Jesus Christ, revealed Himself to me and forgave me so much, I am also extending forgiveness to you and your people."

The nun listened in astonishment; then, her face lines softened, and she began to weep. I extended my arms, and we hugged. We were both weeping and reconciling. Oh, what a glorious moment that neither one will ever forget. The healing flowed from Heaven to both of us.

When you truly forgive, you must first acknowledge the sins committed and give them validity. Then without denial, your choice to forgive will catapult healing into your soul.

> **If we say we have no sin, we are deceiving ourselves and the truth is not in us. If we confess our sins, He is faithful and righteous to forgive our sins and purify us from all unrighteousness. If we say we have not sinned, we make Him a liar and His Word is not in us.**
>
> **1 John 1:8-10**

---

[3]   From Portuguese *auto da fé*, meaning 'act of faith' (Spanish: *auto de fé*) was the ritual of public penance carried out between the 15th and 19th centuries of condemned heretics and apostates imposed by the Spanish, Portuguese, or Mexican Inquisition as punishment and enforced by civil authorities. Its most extreme form was death by burning. (Wikipedia)

It is because of the power of forgiveness as a Jew to the Christians (both Catholics and Protestants) that I have written all my books and especially *The Identity Theft*. I have dedicated my life to expose and uproot the demonic, religious theologies that from the 4th century and on have been established as church doctrine. Because of them, millions of Jews were murdered in the name of Jesus Christ.

It is this awesome force that propelled me to commit my life to bring truth, healing, and deliverance to all the Christian world. I consecrated myself to this Holy work when the Father in Heaven had me lie down on the ash field of the death camp of Auschwitz-Birkenau in Poland. This is where many of my ancestors and my husband's ancestors were exterminated. The God of Israel spoke to me: "This is your pulpit, your altar; you preach from here where the blood of your people is crying for vengeance from the ground."

> Then (YHVH) Adonai said to Cain, "Where is Abel, your brother?" "I don't know," he said. "Am I my brother's keeper?" Then He said, "What have you done? The voice of your brother's blood is crying out to Me from the ground."
>
> **Genesis 4:9-10**

He showed me that I am the prophetic voice of those ashes, and I prayed for Holy revenge so that every drop of Jewish blood spilled on this ground will become a soul saved, delivered, and healed! I have stood in the gap for nearly three decades for the deliverance of all of Christendom from the replacement theology, from the religious system that murdered my people.[4]

It is the power of forgiveness that has taken me to more than 50 nations and hundreds of cities calling Christians to return to the original gospel made in Zion, to the Lion of Judah, to the Jewish Messiah Yeshua, to the Living Torah and Spirit, and to make restitution to the people of Israel and all Jews for the sins committed. Had I not been fully surrendered to the power of forgiveness, I would be crying out revenge and judgment and death to the Christians. But instead, I am crying for repentance, awakening, revival, and the harvest of sheep nations.

I have laid down my life to bring life to those who brought mostly death to us Jews. My book *The Identity Theft* is my gift to all of you. It is the result of over thirty years of ministry bringing truth, light, and healing to your nations. May repentance and forgiveness flow as you accept my gift and read it for yourself. Then pay it forward by gifting it to others.[5]

He entered into the Holies once for all—not by the blood of goats and calves but by His own blood, having obtained eternal redemption.

Hebrews 9:12

I invite you to follow my example, forgive and release from your judgment all those who have wounded you, abused you, betrayed you, and disappointed you. I invite you to be *free* from bitterness!

---

[4]   For more information on this subject, read *The Voice of These Ashes*; available at www.zionsgospel.com

[5]   www.against-antisemitism.com

PRAYER

Yes, Abba, I acknowledge the pain that I have suffered at the hand of (all the names here) because of what he/she did to me. I do not sweep these evil deeds under the carpet, but I expose and denounce them as evil and painful. However, I choose to forgive them, just like You forgave me much because of Yeshua, and I release them from my judgments, including myself and You, Father, in Yeshua's name. I ask You now to heal me in spirit, soul, and body now that the curse and the judgment of bitterness is broken off from my life. Amen.

CHAPTER SIX

Holy and Clean for Life!

> Also anyone the person with the discharge
> touches without rinsing his hands in water
> should wash his clothes and bathe himself in
> water, and be unclean until the evening.
>
> Leviticus 15:11

UNTIL 1980, THE washing of hands was not part of the
health care of America, but the laws of hygiene were part
of the ancient Israelites as far as four thousand years ago!

Surgeons began regularly scrubbing up in the 1870s,
but the importance of everyday handwashing did not
become universal until more than a century later. It
wasn't until the 1980s that hand hygiene was officially
incorporated into American health care with the
first national hand hygiene guidelines. More than a
century after Semmelweis's theories were mocked,
the Medical University of Budapest changed its name
to Semmelweis University, in honor of his unsung

persistence to improve healthcare through cleanliness.[6]

Many women were dying in childbirth because the doctors touched their intimate parts during pregnancy checkups and childbirth with unwashed hands. Doctors would dissect a corpse, and then, with the same hands full of violent bacteria, they would assist in childbirth. Until the late 19th century, it was very dangerous for a woman to give birth in a hospital. Women and babies died by the droves! The simple fact of cleanliness (that all Jews have known since the Torah was given) had escaped the Christian Western culture altogether, as the Jewish Roots of the Faith were rejected by Christendom. Rejecting the Torah and the laws of the God of Israel has cost the lives of millions!

HYGIENE

> So you are to keep Bnei-Yisrael (Children of Israel) separate from their uncleanness, so they will not die in their uncleanness by defiling My Tabernacle that is in their midst.
>
> **Leviticus 15:31**

YHVH gave the ancient Israelites instructions that kept Israel healthier than other nations. Among them were many about bathing, preventing infection, and hygiene. I suggest you show-

---

6   https://www.nationalgeographic.com/history/2020/03/hand-washing-once-controversial-medical-advice/#:~:text=Surgeons%20 began%20regularly%20scrubbing%20up,first%20national%20hand%20hy-giene%20guidelines.

er often, wash your hands before you eat and certainly after you have been in the toilet, wash your clothes often, brush your teeth at least twice a day (including your tongue where most bacteria reside), and maintain a high level of hygiene in your house (including bathroom, kitchen, and refrigerator). Throw away old food; do not keep tins open in the fridge as it can cause botulism, and the poisoned food can kill you. Eat your food fresh. This prevents disease and unnecessary infections.

THE LAW OF NIDDAH

> If a woman has a discharge, and her discharge from her body is blood, she should be in her *niddah* seven days. And whoever touches her will be unclean until the evening. Everything that she lies on in her *niddah* will become unclean. Also everything that she sits on will become unclean.
> **Leviticus 15:19-20**

Women during their period were commanded to have no marital relations and to separate from their husbands for one week. Religious Jewish women that keep this law have no cervical cancer. Women that perform marital sex during the period are at risk of miscarriages and cervical cancer. It is highly displeasing to the Creator for a woman to be penetrated by her husband when bleeding. I suggest you repent of this and learn to separate bodily during your period.

Wash and Be Clean; Immorality Keeps You Dirty, Sick, and Lost for Eternity!

> Or don't you know that the unrighteous will not inherit the Kingdom of God? Don't be deceived! The sexually immoral (including pornography!), idolaters, adulterers, those who practice homosexuality, thieves, the greedy, drunkards, slanderers, swindlers—none of these will inherit the Kingdom of God. That is what some of you were—but you were washed, you were made holy, you were set right in the name of the Lord Yeshua the Messiah and by the Ruach (Spirit) of our God.
>
> 1 Corinthians 6:9-11

Walk in holiness, and you will be healthy! Countless people are sick because of fornication - some with syphilis, others with AIDS, others with problems in the sexual, internal, and reproductive organs because of abortions. Moreover, all addicts, including smokers, are sick in their minds, hearts, and bodies because of their addictions. Many alcoholics are diabetic and have cirrhosis of the liver. All those practicing any kind of immorality are under the curse, and this can bring a host of diseases! Those that are in sin and immorality will be more susceptible to plagues.

Adonai will send on you cursing, confusion and frustration in every undertaking of your hand that you will do—until you are destroyed and perish quickly, because of the evil of your deeds by which you have abandoned Me. Adonai will make the plague cling to you, until He has put an end to you from the land that you are going in to possess. Adonai will strike you with weakness, fever, inflammation, fiery heat, the sword, blight and mildew—they will pursue you until you perish.

Deuteronomy 28:20-22

But when we walk with Yeshua in obedience, holiness, and purity, we have *life* more abundantly!

The thief comes only to steal, slaughter, and destroy. I have come that they might have life, and have it abundantly!

John 10:10

A Holy life unto Yeshua is a healthy life on earth, as well as eternal life in the Creator's presence forever.

Pursue shalom with everyone, and the holiness without which no one will see the Lord.

Hebrews 12:14

PRAYER

Yes, Abba, I embrace Your laws and instructions of morality, cleanliness, and hygiene, and I repent for all immorality and uncleanness, including having relations during my (or my wife's) period in Yeshua's name. Thank you for purifying me from the effects of breaking your instructions in ignorance and delivering me from all the unclean spirits that have plagued my life. Amen.

CHAPTER SEVEN

The Dietary Commandments

> Or don't you know that your body is a temple of
> the Ruach HaKodesh who is in you, whom you
> have from God, and that you are not your own?
> For you were bought with a price. Therefore
> glorify God in your body.
>
> 1 Corinthians 6:19-20

HAVE YOU EVER heard the saying, "You are what you eat"? It is true: whatever type of food, whether good or bad, that you have sown into your body, you will eventually reap. Your cells are made of the stuff you eat, coupled with the way you think and your attitudes. The whole world was up in arms because of the death toll of COVID-19, but people were dying of heart disease four times more than of COVID-19, yet no one has banned the culprits for heart disease. No one has forbidden the use of refined white sugar, white refined flour and grains, MSG, chemical food dyes, full fat meats, pork, and the like. Why is that? Because many companies would be losing money by not selling those items, and money speaks much more than health or truth in this greedy society!

If you follow the principles in the previous six chapters of this book, you will be in much better shape; and, if you change your nutrition to Biblical and commonsense nutrition, your body and soul will be much happier.

Elohim gave clear instructions in the Bible as to what animals to eat and what animals not to eat. He called some of them "detestable," and He surely knows better, as He created them to be ecological cleaners and garbage disposers. He gave His people clear instructions in the Torah to keep them holy (separated from evil) and healthy.

> Adonai spoke to Moses and to Aaron, saying to them, "Speak to Bnei-Yisrael, saying: These are the living things which you may eat among all the animals that are on the earth. Whatever has a split, divided hoof and chews cud among the animals—that you may eat.
>
> Nevertheless, you should not eat of those that only chew cud, or have a split hoof. The camel, though it chews the cud, does not have a divided hoof, is unclean to you. The coney, though it chews the cud yet does not have a divided hoof, so it is unclean to you. The hare, though it chews the cud, does not split the hoof, so it is unclean to you. The pig, though it has a split, divided hoof, does not chew cud, so it is unclean to you. You are not to eat meat from them, nor are you to touch their carcasses. They are unclean to you.
>
> From all that are in the waters, you may eat whatever has fins and scales, within the waters, in the seas and in the rivers. Those you may eat.

But any that do not have fins and scales in the seas or the rivers, among those that swarm on the waters, or among any of the living creatures that are in the waters, they are loathsome to you. They are to be detestable to you. You shall not eat meat from them and you should detest their carcasses. Whatever has neither fins nor scales in the waters, that is a detestable thing to you."

Leviticus 11:1-12

PORK CONSUMPTION

Pork consumption has been proven to put people at risk of hepatitis E, multiple sclerosis, liver cancer, cirrhosis, and yersinia.

Each year in the United States, an estimated 525 000 infections, 2900 hospitalizations, and 82 deaths are attributed to consumption of pork. We analyzed the epidemiology of outbreaks attributed to pork in the United States reported to the Centers for Disease Control and Prevention (CDC) 1998-2015.[7]

Although not a big surprise, the 2017-2021 Production Analysis Summary for the U.S. Pork Industry revealed a continued mortality increase across all production phases. Sow death loss was at 12.6% and continues to be elevated compared to historical levels of 11.1% in 2017.[8]

---

[7]   https://pubmed.ncbi.nlm.nih.gov/28903784/#:~:text=Each%20 year%20in%20the%20United,(CDC)%201998%2D2015.

[8]   https://www.porkbusiness.com/news/hog-production/mortality-continues-challenge-pork-producers

Pork and Multiple Sclerosis

One of the most surprising risks associated with pork — one that's received remarkably little airtime — is multiple sclerosis (MS), a devastating autoimmune condition involving the central nervous system.

In fact, when all countries were considered, pork intake and MS showed a whopping correlation of 0.87 (p<0.001), which is much higher and more significant than the relationship between MS and fat intake (0.63, p<0.01), MS and total meat intake (0.61, p<0.01) and MS and beef consumption (no significant relationship).[9] This correlation coefficient of 0.87 is extremely high, and a p-value below 0.001 also shows a very strong relationship. Thus, MS is much more likely to befall pork eaters. Such a strong correlation makes it look like pork or something found in pork, is the cause of MS.

While pork-averse nations like Israel and India have been nearly spared from MS's degenerative grips, more liberal consumers, such as West Germany and Denmark, face sky-high rates.

Pork Consumption and Liver Cirrhosis

Pork consumption has a strong epidemiological association with cirrhosis of the liver. Startlingly, pork may be even more strongly associated with alcoholic cirrhosis than alcohol itself!

Pork and Liver Cancer

We would expect that if pork can cause liver cirrhosis, it will also promote liver cancer since injured and inflamed tissues

---

[9]   https://www.healthline.com/nutrition/is-porkbad#TOC_TI-TLE_HDR_4

are more likely to become cancerous.

Indeed, there is an association between pork consumption and primary liver cancer, hepatocellular carcinoma.[10]

Contrary to what many believe, the trichina worm present in pork does not die easily, not even in high heat, and it lodges inside the cells of your body as a potential disease ready to explode. Many are sick with chronic diseases, including diabetes, because of pork ingestion. Your gut becomes filthy because of ingesting pork and other unclean animals; the parasites they bring cause a myriad of diseases.

Let Us Take a Closer Look at Shellfish

The following excerpt and testimony from a former shellfish eater explain the hazards quite well.

My dislike for shellfish during pregnancy, including the instructions to avoid certain foods, sparked my curiosity. So, I began to do some research. I had always heard that the first testament of the Bible forbids the consumption of shellfish, but I never gave it much thought. It turns out that they were on to something back then.

You see, shellfish was regarded as "unclean" and for good reason! Shellfish are bottom feeders and consume parasites, including the dead skin of other dead fish. This means that they can contain harmful organisms, including pesticides.

Besides this obvious fact that most people already seem to

---

[10] https://www.psychologytoday.com/us/blog/perfect-health-diet/201202/is-pork-still-dangerous?amp

know, there are a number of other reasons why I completely gave up shellfish.

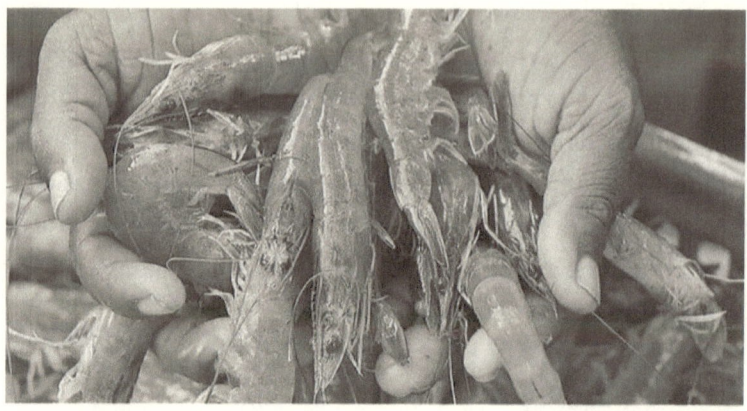

1. Shellfish aren't able to properly expel waste, which can be blamed on their highly simplified digestive system. This is why it is so important to de-vein a shrimp before consumption, as doing so gets rid of the sand and waste contained within it. Gross!
2. Unlike regular fish, shellfish tend to be high in cholesterol. One serving of shrimp alone contains more than half of the daily recommended limit of cholesterol.

3. Consuming spoiled shellfish can be extremely hazardous, leading to food poisoning and a serious bacterial infection. This is why it's so imperative to make sure that it's fresh before consuming.

4. Because shellfish are bottom feeders, they are twice as likely to contain food illnesses (such as salmonella, Norwalk virus, E. coli, and hepatitis A) than their fin and scale counterparts (regular fish). They literally eat all the garbage that is thrown in the ocean...what?!

5. Shellfish contain high levels of mercury, which is one of the most dangerous heavy metals and can cause a plethora of health problems.

6. Shellfish are among the highest allergy-causing foods, and intolerance to them is quite common worldwide.

7. Due to the lack of an adequate digestive system, shellfish cannot easily flush toxins and parasites out of their

system. This means that anyone eating it will then consume the unwanted garbage from the sea as well. Oh, say it isn't so!

8. They are literally insects of the sea; although not directly related, there are some similarities in body structure, making them, well, distant cousins. I am literally shuttering at the thought ... [11]

I could fill this book with data about the toxicity of the animals that He calls "detestable," but I want you to exercise the principle presented in the preamble of this book from John 10:10, which states,

> **The thief comes only to steal, slaughter, and destroy. I have come that they might have life, and have it abundantly!**
>
> **John 10:10**

---

[11]   https://www.projectlifewellness.com/2016/09/28/heres-why-you-should-never-eat-shellfish-again/

You cannot expect an abundance of life when you break the laws of the Creator. He created the animals; some He called "clean" and some "unclean." Noah knew about this, and he brought to the Ark seven of the clean animals and two of the unclean animals.

> **Of every clean animal you shall take with you seven of each kind, male and female; and of the animals which themselves are not clean two, male and female;**
>
> **Genesis 7:2**

It is YHVH who established the creational fact that those animals that chew the cud *and* split the hoof are for human consumption and are called "clean" (such as sheep, goat, cow, deer, and so on). And that those that have one of those mechanisms missing are called "unclean" (such as the pig, the rabbit, the horse, the camel, and more).

It is He who created the fish with scales and fins that could be eaten (such as tuna, sardines, bass, salmon, trout, tilapia, and so on). But those who are missing scales or fins are called detestable (such as catfish, shellfish, oysters, shrimp, octopus, etc.).

It is He who said that carnivorous birds such as the ostrich, vultures, eagles, and ravens are unclean. And the vegetarian ones such as duck, chicken, goose, and turkey are clean.

Christian Replacement Theology has misinterpreted the Word greatly about this subject by misleading people to believe that obeying Yah's Commandments is bondage. By doing so, misled ministers have influenced people wrongly, and they have become sick because of what they eat.

All Scripture is inspired by God and useful for teaching, for reproof, for correction, and for training in righteousness.

2 Timothy 3:16

When Paul wrote the letters to Timothy during the 1st Century AD, the only word available was Holy Scriptures, the Tanakh, which many wrongly call the Old Testament. Doctrine was only based upon what *YHVH* said to the people of Israel interpreted by the Holy Spirit. There was no New Testament from which to read. Paul was saying to Timothy, "Use the Torah and the Prophets to teach the believers - everything you need is there."

In the light of this fact, now you will understand how the Scripture below has been manipulated doctrinally as if it meant that prayer can sanctify even unclean animals, fat, or blood.

For everything created by God is good, and nothing is to be rejected if it is received with thanksgiving; for it is sanctified through the Word of God and prayer.

1 Timothy 4:4-5

Prayer alone cannot sanctify; prayer must be based and ruled by the Word of Yah. He clearly said that when people put a deaf ear to His Laws, to His Torah instructions, their prayer will be an abomination.

One who turns his ear from hearing *Torah* — even his prayer is an abomination.

Proverbs 28:9

If you eat as prescribed by Yah's Commandments, you may pray and, even if there is something wrong in the food, you will be supernaturally protected. This does not apply if you are eating unclean animals, as He warned that they are detestable. People are sick spiritually and physically because of this.

Eating the blood of animals when they are not killed but rather are strangled is another issue. In some societies (like in Germany with the blood sausages and in the Far East with their blood pudding and soup), people are spiritually and physically sick and under curses stemming from violating the laws of the Creator.

> **Anyone from the house of Israel, or from the outsiders dwelling among them, who eats any kind of blood, I will set my face against that soul—the one who eats blood—and will cut him off from among his people. 11 For the life of the creature is in the blood, and I have given it to you on the altar to make atonement for your lives— for it is the blood that makes atonement because of the life. Therefore I have said to *Bnei-Yisrael*: No person among you may eat blood, nor may any outsider dwelling among you eat blood.**
>
> **Leviticus 17:10-12**

Also, many people are dying of heart disease and of clogged arteries because they violate the Commandments about the fat of an animal.

> **It is to be a perpetual statute throughout your generations in all your dwellings, that you must**

eat neither fat nor blood.

                                        Leviticus 3:17

He is to take all its fat from it, and burn it up as
smoke on the altar.

                                        Leviticus 4:19

ANIMAL FAT AND HEART DISEASE

What causes high cholesterol production in the liver? The
answer lies in the types of foods we eat. Diets high in animal
protein and saturated fat have been shown to increase cholesterol. The cholesterol-raising effect of saturated fat and the
links with heart disease are well-documented. All major health
organizations (WHO, American Dietetic Association, Dieti-
tians of Canada, British Dietetic Association, American Heart
Association, British Heart Foundation, World Heart Federa-
tion, British National Health Service, US Food and Drug Ad-
ministration, and European Food Safety Authority) agree that
saturated fat is a risk factor for heart disease.[12]

By the way, in 2019 alone, over 700,000 people died in the
USA from heart disease! This is 4 times more than COVID-19
in one year!

As I sum up this important chapter, I hope that you will
implement the instructions of the Creator and treat Him with
honor and respect by honoring your body, which is the Tem-
ple of the Holy Spirit.

---

[12]   https://www.vivahealth.org.uk/resources/meat-truth/
truth-about-saturated-fat-animal-protein-and-cholesterol-online

PRAYER

Abba, Father, I ask Your forgiveness for my ignorance and for breaking Your Dietary Laws and instructions. I have polluted my body with things You call detestable. I repent and turn back to Your ways in my food habits and renounce all unclean, unbiblical eating in Yeshua's name. I empty my fridge and freezer from all those things that are an affront to You, and I surrender to Your dietary instructions for holiness and wellbeing. Thank You for setting me free from all the curses and diseases, even the one hiding in my cells due to my unclean, lustful, ignorant eating in Yeshua's name. Amen.

CHAPTER EIGHT

Wine or No Wine, that is the Question

"Amen, I tell you, I will never again drink of the fruit of the vine, until that day when I drink it anew in the kingdom of God."

Mark 14:25 TLV

WE CAN SEE that Yeshua did not oppose drinking the fruit of the vine, which mistakenly is equated to the commercial product you can find in the shops nowadays. The wine of the Biblical era was much weaker than the wine we know today. While one reason for this was the addition of water, another reason was that naturally fermented wine (wine that does not have additives) was the only wine available during this time. Wine made in biblical times underwent a much simpler process, grown and produced naturally without chemical processing or anything being added or removed. It would have tasted quite different from the wine we enjoy today that is full of chemicals and additives but was perhaps more like fermented grape juice.

Why Was Yeshua Given Wine Mixed with Gall?

Gall refers to a substance made from Myrrh, which was mixed into the wine offered to Yeshua the first time. Yeshua tasted it and realized that this concoction was designed to dull his senses and ease some of the pain from his crucifixion. Aside from that, the combination is narcotic, which could have been given to him in an attempt to end his life and suffering sooner.

The second wine was offered to him in a sponge, and the wine was sour. Sour wine in Roman times was used as a refreshing way to quench their thirst. It is presumed that the bystander who offered him this sour wine did so to extend the time he was awake and thus his suffering.

Old Wine and New Wine

Old wine is fermented and has an alcoholic content. The new wine mentioned in the Bible is usually grape juice and has little or no alcoholic content.

The strongest alcoholic beverage that was accessible to the New Testament authors and their original readers was natural wine that had an alcoholic content of 11-12 percent (before dilution). Also, ancient wine was normally diluted before drinking, probably to an alcohol content of 5-8%, both to avoid too much intoxication and to make it last.

Do you wonder why people find themselves "tipsy" after just one glass of wine? As it turns out, wine is stronger than it used to be, as strong as 14-20% alcohol, and people that drink do not dilute it; thus, it can cause much more addiction and alcoholism. Additionally, a joint study by Cornell and Iowa State universities found that the size and shape of a glass can affect how much people pour in various circumstances. One glass of chardonnay could be all it takes to cause a deadly drunk driving crash. [13]

The Bible talks a lot about wine's beneficial properties as well as its dangers when abused.

> "They hit me! But I was not hurt. They beat me up! But I did not feel it. When will I wake up? I will look for another drink."
>
> Proverbs 23:35 TLV

Many of the car accidents in the USA today are because of DUI, driving under the influence of the commercial wine or another form of alcohol that is popular today, e.g., beer or other spirits. Many families throughout the world have been torn apart because of alcoholism. Many children have been abused and even raped by alcoholic parents under the influence of wine or another form of alcohol.

A recent study by the Centers for Disease Control and Prevention (CDC) found that, while guns are indeed responsible for more fatalities overall, drunk driving actually kills more people on a per capita basis.[14] In other words, you are more likely to be killed by a drunk driver than by a gun.

Most of the work-related accidents are caused by drug or alcohol abuse.

The U.S. Department of Labor claims that 65% of on-the-job accidents are related to drug and alcohol abuse in the

---

[13]   https://usa-law.org/can-i-drive-after-one-glass-of-wine/

[14]   https://www.davidazizipersonalinjury.com/is-it-more-dangerous-to-be-killed-by-a-drunk-driver-or-a-gun/#:~:text=A%20recent%20study%20by%20the,driver%20than%20by%20a%20gun.

workplace. According to the Addiction Center, "drinking on the job can also lead to aggravated assault and sexual battery charges," resulting in higher healthcare costs for any employees affected second handedly. Not only is your company going to face financial issues, but company employees become at-risk and experience a lower level of safety at work.[15]

According to a paper by the American Society of Addiction Medicine (ASAM), different studies have found that substance misuse is involved in 40% to 60% of the reported incidents of domestic violence. Additionally, more than 20% of male offenders report using alcohol prior to their most recent and severe violent acts.[16]

For those of you that excuse your wine or alcohol addiction by saying that the Bible sanctions drinking wine, please be aware that you have misinterpreted the Scriptures and not heeded its warnings. Your addiction to wine and any alcohol may cost you your kingdom inheritance for eternity!

> **"Or don't you know that the unrighteous will not inherit the kingdom of God? Don't be deceived! The sexually immoral, idolaters, adulterers, those who practice homosexuality, thieves, the greedy, drunkards, slanderers, swindlers—none of these will inherit the kingdom of God."**
>
> **1 Corinthians 6:9-10**

---

[15]   https://ondemandoccupationalmedicine.com/addiction-in-the-workplace/#:~:text=The%20U.S.%20Department%20of%20Labor,alcohol%20abuse%20in%20the%20workplace.

[16]   https://alcohol.org/women/domestic-abuse-and-alcoholism/#

We have already established that the wine you drink is not the same as the Biblical wine. If you insist on drinking this commercial substance called "wine" today, at least do yourself and your loved ones a favor: Dilute it by two thirds, so you have one third commercial wine and two thirds water. This will decrease your addiction and prevent serious problems.

Remember that Yeshua invites us to become a new wine skin for the new wine that does not intoxicate but rather nourishes, as it has either no alcohol content or extremely low alcohol content. However, He said that people prefer the high alcohol content and reject the new wine.

> **"No man who drinks old wine wants new, because he says, 'The old is fine.'"**
> **Luke 5:39 TLV**

Recall that old wine was fermented grape juice, while new wine is what we call grape juice today.

> **"They have eaten but will not be satisfied. They have fornicated but will not increase. For they stopped giving heed to Adonai. Prostitution and wine—even new wine— it takes away understanding."**
> **Hosea 4:10-11 TLV**

In Hebrew, old wine is the word *Yain* while the word for new wine is *Tirosh,* which is nonalcoholic grape juice. The Holy Spirit is likened unto this new wine. We must keep drinking of Him to stay fresh and vibrant in our walk with Him. We are warned not to get drunk with wine.

"And do not get drunk on wine, for that is recklessness. Instead, be filled with the Ruach,"

Ephesians 5:18 TLV

It is not a sin to drink a small amount of fermented wine. It is a sin to abuse it.

Some of us are called, like the Sons of Rechab, not to drink any alcohol.

"The words of Jonadab son of Rechab, that he commanded his sons, not to drink wine, are observed, and to this day they drink none, for they listen to their father's commandment. Yet I have spoken to you, early and often, and you have not obeyed Me."

Jeremiah 35:14

Also, John the Baptizer was commanded to be a Nazarite by not drinking any fruit of the vine. The yeast in the air will cause fermentation and alcohol even in the grape juice.

"Speak to Bnei-Yisrael and say to them: Any man or woman who desires to vow a Nazirite vow to be separate for Adonai, is to abstain from wine and any other fermented drink. He is not to drink any vinegar made from wine or any fermented drink, or any grape juice, or eat grapes or raisins."

Numbers 6:23

And remember that priests were not allowed into the Holy Place after drinking any form of wine or alcohol.

"Do not drink wine or fermented drink, neither you nor your sons with you, when you go into the Tent of Meeting, so that you do not die. This is to be a statute forever throughout your generations."

Leviticus 10:9

Kings were advised not to rule when drinking fermented grape juice or other strong drinks.

"It is not for kings, O Lemuel, it is not for kings to drink wine, or for rulers to crave strong drink, lest they drink, forget what is decreed, and pervert justice for all the oppressed."

Proverbs 31:4-5

Noah lost his modesty and dignity when he made himself fermented wine from the grapes he planted. This brought a curse to the son of Ham and his generations.

"Then Noah, a man of the soil, was first to plant a vineyard. He drank some of the wine, got drunk, and was uncovered in his tent."

Genesis 9:20-21

When considering whether to drink or not to drink wine, or any other alcoholic beverage, please submit yourself to the Ruach HaKodesh (Holy Spirit) within you and see what His leading is over your life.

"For if you live according to the flesh, you must die; but if by the Ruach you put to death the

deeds of the body, you shall live. For all who are
led by the Ruach Elohim, these are sons of God."

Romans 8:13-14

And when in doubt, then do not drink. It is safer that way
and you will not be harmed if you do not drink. And if you
are permitted by Yah to drink occasionally and your drinking
causes others to stumble, then refrain from drinking at all in
front of them.

> **"But watch out that this freedom of yours does
> not somehow become a stumbling block to the
> weak."**
>
> **1 Corinthians 8:9**

The Biblical kind of naturally fermented grape juice wine
may be beneficial in measure. Paul advised this to Timothy:

> **"(No longer drink only water, but use a little
> wine for your stomach and for your frequent
> ailments.)"**
>
> **1 Timothy 5:23**

But please remember that this wine was not the commercial product of today. It was naturally fermented grapes, and
it was diluted. Paul was saying to add a little fermented grape
juice to your water. You must be honest with yourself and be
led by the Spirit as in every area of your life.

> **"... so that the requirement of the Torah might
> be fulfilled in us, who do not walk according to
> the flesh but according to the Ruach."**
>
> **Romans 8:4**

He may lead you to:

1. Not drink wine or alcohol at all.
2. Make your own fermented grape juice at home to use occasionally.
3. He may allow you to drink a very small amount during celebrations and occasions.
4. He may allow you to drink a super diluted glass of commercial wine occasionally.
5. He may only let you cook with it.

Make sure you obey Him as it will save you, your loved ones and humanity as a whole an untold amount of embarrassment and woes. It can even save you from eternal damnation.

> "Everything is permitted for me"—but not everything is helpful. "Everything is permitted for me"—but I will not be controlled by anything."
>
> **1 Corinthians 6:12**

Warning:

If you are addicted and cannot live without your wine, beer, or any alcoholic drink, you need to STOP and confess it to someone that walks with Yah in holiness and power and ASK for prayer!

> "Therefore, openly acknowledge your sins to one another, and pray for each other, so that you may be healed. The prayer of a righteous person is powerful and effective."
>
> **Ya'akov (Jas) 5:16 CJB**

If you want to get rid of your addiction to wine and alcohol, kneel where you are and ask forgiveness from YHVH in the name of Yeshua. Then reject your addiction out loud, remove all wine and alcohol from your house and resist the temptation until it leaves you. Ask the Ruach HaKodesh to help you and He will!

> **"Submit yourselves therefore to God. Resist (and keep resisting) the devil, and he will (eventually) flee from you."**
>
> Ya'akov (Jas) 4:7

I strongly advise that you take our GRM Bible School[17] which I call "The Heavenly Washing Machine", as it will equip you in the faith and help you to start afresh.

> **"I will lift up the cup of salvation, and call on the Name of YHVH."**
>
> Psalms 116:13 STB

Lechayim! To life!

---

17   www.grmbibleinstitute.com

CHAPTER NINE

Food for Life!

Then *ADONAI Elohim* caused to sprout from the
ground every tree that was desirable to look at
and good for food.

Genesis 2:9

IN THIS CHAPTER, I will give you a principle that can guide
you for life: The closer your food is to the way it was created
by Elohim, the better. Whenever you go shopping, avoid processed foods and instead go to the fruit and vegetables department. Raw fruits, raw vegetables, raw nuts, sprouted lentils
and beans, whole grains, unrefined sugars, or fruit sugars and
date sugars would be the best choice.

For protein, you can choose a combination of whole grains
with beans, clean fish (such as tuna, tilapia, salmon, trout, sea
bass, sardines, etc.), lean meats, organic eggs, or egg whites,
and lean cheeses.

Avoid white sugar at all costs. When I was exercising my
nutrition profession, we used to call white sugar "white poison," the same title as for the drug heroin. White sugar is refined like heroin, and it is highly addictive. White sugar is a
silent killer behind many diseases starting from the gut. It kills

the good bacteria of the gut, and it causes the bad ones to pro-
liferate; it causes constipation, candida, cancer, heart disease,
and an impeded immune system.

Sugar hides in nearly every packaged food in the supermar-
ket; therefore, you need to check labels and choose the foods
with zero or very little added sugar - zero is best. All fruits have
healthy fruit sugar, and that should be enough to sweeten your
life. Raw sugar cane is a much better choice than white sugar -
so is honey, agave, monk fruit, and stevia. Just escape the white
sugar at the speed of light! If you are craving something sweet,
have a date or a teaspoon of raw honey on a whole rice cracker.

Avoid empty carbs! Those are the carbs that give you no vitamins, cause constipation (for lack of fiber) and steal vitamins
from your body to digest them. Remember the principle at the
preamble of this book?

> **The thief comes only to steal, slaughter, and
> destroy. I have come that they might have life,
> and have it abundantly!**
>
> **John 10:10**

Here are some examples of empty carbs:
- White sugar
- White bread or enriched bread
- White rice
- White flour as in cakes, pies, cookies, and any dough
- Many of the chips and munchies (snack foods)

Instead of empty carbs, choose these in measure:

- Fruit
- Dates
- Date sugar, coconut sugar, honey, agave, monk fruit, and stevia
- Whole wheat bread (100% whole wheat)
- Multigrain bread without sugar (with whole grain only)
- Whole Spelt bread
- Brown or wild rice
- Quinoa
- Amaranth
- Whole barley
- Whole rice cakes

There is much more to say about the subject, and there are many recipe books out there. Just exercise the principles I give you in this book, and you will be well.

Important tips:

- Avoid gelatin unless it is vegetarian or vegan. Most gelatin is derived from pork or horse, and both are unclean animals.
- Avoid fried foods. They are full of free radicals that cause cancer, and in most restaurants, they are fried in the same oil as shellfish and pork. Eat things raw, steamed, or grilled.
- Avoid refined oils. Oil is a very concentrated food - use it sparingly and choose unrefined olive oil and other unrefined oils that have not been heated or processed. They normally say "cold-pressed."

- Avoid nitrates - these are chemicals used to enhance the color of meat, and they are carcinogenic.
- Avoid food dyes unless they say "natural ingredients."
- Avoid MSG. This is another chemical and flavor enhancer that causes much trouble, including bloating, allergies, and migraine headaches. You will find it predominantly in Chinese and Asian western food.
- Avoid salad dressings. Most of them have lots of sugar and fat. Go for sugar-free and fat-free as much as you can or make your own.
- Avoid milk chocolate: it's highly addictive and full of sugar! Sparingly eat dark chocolate (above 80%) instead. You can make great drinks from 100% organic cacao powder sweetened with stevia or monk fruit (zero calories).
- Avoid sodas - drink water instead! You can treat yourself to sparkling mineral water with natural lemon occasionally. (At least ten to twelve glasses of good water a day is advised)
- Avoid too much coffee or tea! One a day is plenty. Most people are addicted to caffeine, and this can be destructive and even affect your blood pressure. Natural coffee is great if taken in small measures. You can drink herbal teas such as mint, chamomile, lemongrass, and many others that will be beneficial to you.
- Avoid fruit juices: there is too much fruit sugar in them, and you will turn your body acidic and gain weight.
- Avoid drinking milk. Pasteurized milk is not a healthy food. Instead, drink coconut milk, almond milk, or-

ganic non-lactose milk, or goat milk.

- Avoid sugar and all sugared candy.

If you are allergic to gluten, choose gluten-free.
If you are allergic to nuts, do not eat them.
If you are allergic to lactose, choose lactose-free.

VITAMINS AND SUPPLEMENTS

Since we are not in the Garden of Eden, where fruits and seeds were full of vitamins and proteins, it is important to take vitamin supplements. Make sure they are made from natural ingredients (with no added sugar and mostly good for vegans), so you do not have all kinds of unclean ingredients in them. I have taken healthy vitamins, supplements, herbs, and probiotics since my youth, and it has paid off! Find out in prayer and by research what would be good for you.

I normally recommend that everyone take an umbrella of a potent natural vegan multivitamin and mineral supplement, along with additional calcium, magnesium, and vitamin C, especially chewable or drinkable. Oil of oregano in vegetarian capsules is excellent to prevent infection, and so is zinc. Turmeric is wonderful against inflammation and aches and pains. Probiotics + prebiotics are quite mandatory to keep the gut in good shape. Added fiber may be necessary if you are not going to the toilet daily and regularly, but I have noticed that drinking lots of water (about ten to twelve glasses a day) solves many problems. Choose the best water you can, as your body is made of 60% water, so drink good water (spring water, water by reverse osmosis and the like), but absolutely drink water!

There is much more to say about nutrition and health, but I have endeavored to give you principles to help you get healthy. This book is not replacing proper nutritional or medical counseling. It is written for inspiration only. However, if you follow its principles, you may not need to be dependent on the medical system.

An ancient Jewish sage and doctor in the Middle Ages once said,

"Let your food be your medicine."

I believe that the Creator gave us all we need to sustain life and even to become whole. His manual of instructions, the Bible, stands firm through the ages.

Lechayim! To life!

BONUS BAKING RECIPES

But you would be fed with the finest wheat, with honey out of a rock would I satisfy you."
Psalm 81:17

Before I met Yeshua, I was a pioneer of health foods, nutrition, natural childbirth, and breastfeeding in Israel. I had two health food stores and my own clinic. People used to come from all over the land for nutritional counseling. I had written a column in local magazines and some readers even swore that I saved their lives through my knowledge of health, herbs, vitamins, and nutrition.

When I surrendered my life to Yeshua, I wanted to bless the body of Messiah in Israel through my baking. In fact, I thought that was my calling. Yah made sure that I answered another calling, the one He had for me from the beginning of time. This calling was and is to be an emissary, an apostle to the nations, and to "bake" spiritual goods, including preparing prophetic messages, books, and Bible School in order to raise healthy disciples.

> **Yahveh's words are flawless words, as silver refined in a clay furnace, purified seven times.**
> **Psalm 12:6 WEB**

However, my love for baking and for healthy foods never left me. Those of my team who have lived with me can attest to that. These are some of my favorite healthy baking recipes. Enjoy!

IMPORTANT INSTRUCTIONS

Before I bake or cook, I pray, cleanse my heart and mind and tune in to the Holy Spirit. I wash and sanitize my hands thoroughly. I also pray in tongues throughout the baking and cooking process. I often bake while wearing a tallit (prayer mantle). Whatever spirit is in you will go into the food you are preparing, so I make sure that whatever I bake or cook is anointed. The anointing is that added "extra" to any good recipe, and it makes it great!

The Challa is the Shabbat Bread, and it makes the Shabbat dedication dinner on Friday night so much more special. We normally make a mixture of olive oil, crushed garlic, salt, and chopped herbs (representing the anointing of the Holy Spirit) to dip the Challa into when we do this blessing over the bread on Shabbat:

"Baruch Ata Adonai Eloheinu Melech Haolam HaMotsih Lechem Min Haarets"

(Blessed are you YHVH, our God, King of the Universe, who has brought forth bread from the earth.)

I have many different challa recipes; I chose to share three of them with you.

WHOLE WHEAT RAISIN CHALLA

Ingredients:

> 5 teaspoons (2 packages) active dry yeast
> 1/2 cup + 1 Tablespoon brown or raw sugar
>   1 3/4 cups lukewarm water
> 1/2 cup olive oil plus more for greasing the bowl
> 5 large eggs divided
> 1 teaspoon kosher salt, sea salt, or Himalayan salt
> 2 teaspoons cinnamon
> 8 cups whole wheat flour
> 1 cup raisins

Instructions:

- In a large bowl, dissolve the yeast and 1 tablespoon brown sugar in the warm water. Let sit for 5 minutes until foamy.
- Whisk the oil into yeast, then beat in four eggs, one at a time, with remaining ½ cup brown sugar, cinnamon and salt. Gradually add flour and raisins. When the dough holds together, it is ready for kneading. You can also use a mixer with a dough hook for both mixing and kneading, but be careful if using a standard mixer.

- Turn dough onto a floured surface and knead until smooth, about 5-10 minutes. Clean out bowl and grease it, then return dough to bowl. Cover with plastic wrap and let rise in a warm place for one hour, until almost doubled in size. (At this point, you can let the dough sit overnight in the fridge or continue to the next rising.) Punch down dough, cover, and let rise again in a warm place for another half-hour. (Again, at this point, you can let the dough sit overnight in the fridge or continue to the next rising.)
- To make a three-braid challa, divide the dough in half and place one half in the oiled bowl, and cover. Take the remaining half of the dough and form it into three balls. With your hands, roll each ball into a strand about 12 inches long and 1 1/2 inches wide. Pinch the tops of the strands together. Bring the right outside rope over the center rope; that rope now becomes the center. Bring the left outside rope over the new center rope; that rope now becomes the center. Continue braiding until you reach the end. Pinch the ropes together to seal.
- If baking immediately, preheat oven to 375 degrees F (190 degrees C). Beat the remaining egg and brush it on the loaves. Allow the bread to rise another hour or place it in the fridge to rise overnight.
- When ready to bake, brush loaves again with the egg wash. Sprinkle bread with sesame or chia seeds or oat flakes, if desired. Bake in the middle of the oven for 30 to 40 minutes, or until golden. Cool loaves on a rack.
- The bread can be frozen, unbaked, or baked. Enjoy on Shabbat!

SIMPLE WHOLE WHEAT CHALLA

Original recipe yields 16 servings
(Double the recipe if needed)

Ingredients:

- 4 cups whole wheat flour
- 1 teaspoon salt
- 1 teaspoon cinnamon
- 2 ¼ teaspoons active dry yeast (plus half a tablespoon raw sugar)
- 2 tablespoons ground oats or hemp
- ½ cup honey
- ½ cup olive oil
- 1 cup warm water
- 2 eggs
- ¼ cup raisins, to taste (optional)

Instructions:

Step 1

In a large bowl, put the yeast with one tablespoon of raw sugar and the warm water and let it bubble for 5 minutes. Then add all wet ingredients. Then put all dry ingredients in another bowl and add them to the wet mixture.

Step 2

Turn the dough out onto a floured surface, and knead until smooth and elastic, about 10 minutes. Form the dough into a round shape. Lightly oil a bowl, place the dough in the bowl, and turn the dough over a few times to oil the surface. Cover the bowl with a cloth, and let rise in a warm, draft-free place until doubled, about one hour.

Step 3

Punch down the dough, knead it a few times to remove some of the bubbles, and cut it into two equal-sized pieces. Set one piece of dough aside under a cloth to prevent drying out while you shape or braid the first loaf as desired.

Step 4

Working on a floured surface, roll the small dough pieces into ropes about the thickness of your thumb and about 12 inches long. Ropes should be fatter in the middle and thinner at the ends. Pinch three ropes together at the top and braid them. Starting with the strand to the right, move it to the left, over the middle strand (that strand becomes the new middle strand.) Take the strand farthest to the left and move it over the new middle strand. Continue braiding, alternating sides each time, until the loaf is braided, and pinch the ends together and fold them underneath for a neat look. Repeat for the other loaf, then place the braided loaves on a baking sheet lined with parchment paper, and let rise in a warm place until doubled, about 30 minutes.

Step 5

Preheat oven to 350 degrees F (175 degrees C).

Step 6

Bake in the preheated oven until golden brown, about 30 minutes. Serve warm for best flavor.

Shabbat shalom!

NON-YEAST OAT WHOLE WHEAT MOLDED CHALLA OR BREAD

If cooked on a challa mold, it will be a challa; if you do not have one, just enjoy it as a delicious non-yeast loaf of bread.

Ingredients:
(You can double this recipe for a larger loaf)

> 1 cup rolled oats (ground)
> 1 cup whole wheat flour
> 2 teaspoons baking powder
> ½ teaspoon salt
> 1 teaspoon cinnamon
> 1 ½ tablespoons honey
> 1 tablespoon vegetable oil (coconut or olive)
> 1 cup milk
> ½ cup raising

Instructions:

Step 1
Preheat oven to 450 degrees F (230 degrees C)

Step 2
Grind oatmeal in a food processor or blender. In a large bowl, combine oatmeal, flour, baking powder, and salt. In a separate bowl, dissolve honey in vegetable oil, then stir in the milk. Combine both mixtures, add the raisins (fold into the dough), and stir until a soft dough is formed. Form the dough into a ball and place on a lightly oiled baking sheet or put in Challa mold or bread pan (non-stick pan or sprayed with Pam or lightly oiled).

Step 3

Bake in preheated oven for about 20 minutes, or until bottom of loaf sounds hollow when tapped.

DELICIOUS WHOLE WHEAT BANANA BREAD

Ingredients:

⅓ cup melted coconut oil or extra-virgin olive oil

½ cup honey or maple syrup

2 eggs

1 cup mashed bananas

1 teaspoon vanilla extract

½ teaspoon salt

½ teaspoon cinnamon, plus more to swirl on top

1 ¼ cups whole spelt or whole wheat flour

1 teaspoon baking soda*

¼ cup hot water*

1 cup broken walnuts or pecans (optional)

Instructions:

- Preheat oven to 325 degrees F (165 degrees C) and grease a 9×5-inch loaf pan.
- In a large bowl, beat oil and honey together. Add eggs and beat well.
- Stir in bananas and vanilla, then stir in the salt and cinnamon. Lastly, stir in the flour, just until combined. Add the nuts (optional)
- Add baking soda to hot water, stir to mix, and then mix briefly into batter until it is evenly distributed.

- Spread batter into the greased loaf pan.
- Sprinkle with cinnamon and swirl with a toothpick or the tip of a butter knife for a pretty marbled effect.

Bake for 55 to 65 minutes. Be sure to check that the bread is done baking by inserting a toothpick in the top. It should come out clean. Let the bread cool in the loaf pan for 5 minutes, then transfer it to a wire rack to cool for 30 minutes before slicing.

Yummy Carrot Date Spelt Muffins

Ingredients:

1 cup almond milk
1/4 teaspoon vinegar
1/4 cup liquid coconut oil (not hot)
1 egg
1 teaspoon vanilla
1/4 cup honey
6 large dates finely chopped
10 baby carrots grated (about 1 1/2 cups)
1 3/4 cups spelt flour
1/2 cup ground almonds or hemp
2 teaspoon cinnamon
1/3 cup coconut sugar
1 teaspoon baking powder
1 teaspoon baking soda
1/2 teaspoon coarse sea salt

Instructions:

- Preheat the oven to 350 degrees F (175 degrees C) and line muffin tin with 12 liners.
- Combine milk, vinegar, honey, coconut oil, egg, and vanilla by beating with an electric mixer.
- Add in the chopped dates and grated carrots and mix again.
- In a separate bowl, whisk together the remaining ingredients.
- Add them to the wet mixture and mix until just combined.
- Scoop out the batter, filling muffin liners 3/4 full.
- Bake for 25 minutes, checking that a toothpick comes out clean.
- Let cool on a rack for 20 minutes.

Spelt Pumpkin Muffins

Ingredients:

1 1/2 cups whole spelt flour, can substitute whole-wheat flour

1 tablespoon pumpkin pie spice

1 teaspoon baking soda

1/4 teaspoon baking powder

1/2 teaspoon salt

2 eggs

1/2 cup honey

1/3 cup butter, melted

1 cup pumpkin puree or apple puree or bananas or carrots

1/2 cup raisins

Instructions:

- Preheat the oven to 350 degrees F (175 degrees C). Line a muffin pan with liners and set aside.
- Using a whisk or fork, mix together the flour, pumpkin spice, baking soda, baking powder, and salt.
- Make a well (hole) in the center of the flour mixture and drop in the eggs, honey, and melted butter. Mix together until well combined. Fold in the pumpkin puree. Do not overmix.
- Pour the batter into the muffin pan, so it's evenly distributed. Bake until golden brown and a toothpick comes clean, about 18 – 20 minutes. Store at room temperature or freeze for a rainy day.

MY VEGAN CHOCOLATE SPELT CAKE

Ingredients:

2 cups spelt flour
3/4 cup cocoa powder
1 teaspoon baking soda
1 teaspoon salt
1 cup mini unsweetened chocolate chips, optional
1 1/2 cups raw sugar, monk sugar, or xylitol for
    sugar-free
1/2 cup applesauce, banana, or yogurt of choice plus
    some date honey (2 Tablespoons)
1/2 cup coconut oil, almond butter, or allergy-friendly
    substitute
1 1/2 tablespoons pure vanilla extract
1 1/2 cups water

Instructions:

- Preheat the oven to 350 degrees F (175 degrees C). Grease two 8-inch square or round pans. Set aside.
- Stir together the flour, cocoa powder, baking soda, salt, optional chips, and sweetener in a bowl. (If your nut butter is not stir-able, gently heat until it softens.) In a new bowl, whisk the oil or nut butter, applesauce or yogurt, date honey, water, and vanilla. Pour wet into dry and stir until just combined (don't over-mix). Pour into the pans.
- Bake on the center rack for 25 minutes or until batter has risen and a toothpick inserted into the center of the cakes comes out mostly clean. (I like to take them out when still a little undercooked, let cool, then set in the fridge overnight. This prevents overcooking, and the cakes firm up nicely as they sit.)
- If you can wait, I highly recommend not tasting until the next day... this cake is so much richer and sweeter after sitting for a day! When ready to frost, go around the sides with a knife, then invert each cake onto a large plate. Frost separately, then place one cake on top of the other if a double-layer cake is desired. At this point, you can also frost the sides if you wish.

For the Frosting:

2 cups pitted dates (soaked in warm water to soften if they are hard)

¼ rounded cup raw cacao powder

¼ teaspoon fine sea salt

½ cup almond milk (or rice milk)

2 heaping tablespoons of almond butter

Instructions:

- Add your dates, cacao powder, and salt to your food processor. Blend until small bits remain, then slowly add your almond milk with blender running. Add your almond butter and blend until you have thick and smooth frosting. If the frosting is too thin, add more almond butter. If it is too thick, add more almond milk.
- Spread your date frosting on your completely cooled cake.

(You can make more frosting and spread between the two layers and on top to make it richer. You can exchange almond butter for coconut butter). Beteavon! Bon Appetit!

MASTER TONIC (NON-REFRIGERATED)

This[18] is the Master Tonic I make; all in our home have used it.

Make plenty, as the Master Tonic does not need refrigeration and lasts indefinitely without any special storage conditions. The healthiest Master Tonic is made with homemade apple cider vinegar brewed with raw honey.

If you don't have time to do this, then be sure to buy only raw ACV (apple cider vinegar) packed in glass bottles. Never buy it packaged in plastic, as the acidity of the ACV will leach toxins into the vinegar.

---

[18]   https://www.thehealthyhomeeconomist.com/master-tonic-natural-flu-antiviral/ (Sarah Pope MGA)

Prep Tip

These ingredients can make your eyes water and burn while you are chopping and grating. I put a large cutting board on my (cool) stovetop and turn on the fan above the range on high. This allows me to chop everything without discomfort.

Minimizing Time Spent

I've recently noticed that bags of organic, peeled, whole garlic cloves are available at some health food stores. Using these instead of peeling the garlic yourself will easily halve the time required to make this traditional Tonic. It will also prevent your hands from smelling like garlic for two days!

Nightshade Allergy?

If you are allergic to nightshade vegetables, substitute grated turmeric root for the cayenne pepper or double up on the onion or garlic.

The dosage for the Master Tonic is 1 or 2 ounces, two or more times daily. Swish and swallow.

Don't dilute with water if you can avoid it. Mix with food if you have to, but best to take it full strength on its own.

Master Tonic Recipe

The Master Tonic is a must-have remedy for the flu season or when traveling overseas. It is potently anti-viral, anti-parasitic, anti-bacterial, and anti-fungal. It requires no refrigeration and lasts indefinitely with no special storage conditions.

Prep Time: 45 minutes
Total Time: 45 minutes
Calories 15 kcal

Ingredients
(You can divide and half the quantities to make less)

- 1 cup fresh chopped garlic, preferably organic
- 1 cup fresh chopped onion, preferably organic
- 1 cup fresh grated ginger root, preferably organic
- 1 cup fresh grated horseradish root, preferably organic
- 1 cup fresh chopped cayenne peppers or any hot peppers seasonally available, preferably organic
- 1-quart raw apple cider vinegar
- 1 half-gallon mason jar

Instructions

Fill a half-gallon glass mason jar 3/4 of the way full with equal parts by volume of the above fresh chopped and grated herbs (1 cup each works well). Wear gloves when chopping the hot peppers.

Organic Master Tonic ingredients

Fill the jar to the top with raw ACV (apple cider vinegar). Close the lid tightly and shake.

Fermenting Master Tonic ingredients

Shake at least once a day for two weeks, and then filter the Master Tonic mixture through a clean piece of cloth, bottle, and label.

Make sure that when you make this Tonic, you shake it every time you walk by it, a minimum of once per day.

Recipe Notes

Use only fresh and preferably organically grown herbs, if possible, as this will make the most potent and effective Master

Tonic. Substitute dried bulk herbs only in an emergency if fresh is unavailable.

If one of the ingredients is not available (fresh horseradish is difficult during certain times of the year), substitute another hot pepper such as habanero.

Nutrition Facts

Master Tonic Recipe
Amount Per Serving (1 Tbsp)
Calories 15
% Daily Value[19]

- Potassium 11mg0%
- Carbohydrates 3.5g1%

---

[19]   Percent Daily Values are based on a 2000 calorie diet.

Extra Information

Though I have walked in divine health since I met the Messiah, by faith in His Word and the power of His Ruach, keeping my heart and mind as clean and pure as possible, I have also taken natural vitamins and supplements since my 20's that no doubt have helped. My former training as a nutritionist and health consultant (probably some of the best in Israel in the 80's!) has been a great blessing to many around the globe. *Keep your immune system in top shape!* Above *all*, utilize the power of His Word, and take advantage of natural help. I like to "shoot" the enemy with all the bullets and weapons I have!

> **The thief comes only to steal and kill and destroy; I came so that they would have life and have it abundantly.**
>
> John 10:10

IMPORTANT FOR IMMUNE SYSTEM

Here are some suggestions for maintaining a healthy immune system:[20]
(NOTE: All capsules - not tablets - need to be vegan to avoid pork gelatin and shellfish.)

---

[20]   For general information only

- Vitamin D 5000 IU (K2+D3)
- Zinc 40 Mg
- Pro biotic 50 billion
- Quercetin 500 to 1000 mg
- Solgar VM75 vegan multi vitamin and mineral with high B and A
- (Vitamin C 1000 mgs a day)
  - Two or three times a week I take Vitamin C powder 5000 mgs
  - If there are any symptoms of the flu, cold, or any disease, then take every day until diarrhea begins, then stop until diarrhea stops and start again with half dose until completely well.
- NAC, a potent antioxidant

I believe in prevention both spiritually, physically, and emotionally, rather than treatment. Be prepared! We have only one life and one body to serve Him with. Proclaim the Word, take charge over your body by exercising authority, and teach others to do the same!

SPIRITUAL AND NATURAL PREVENTION

Therefore I urge you, brothers and sisters, by the mercies of God, to present your bodies as a living and holy sacrifice, acceptable to God, which is your spiritual service of worship. And do not be conformed to this world, but be transformed by the renewing of your mind, so that you may prove what the will of God is, that which is good and acceptable and perfect.

Romans 12:1-2

And He said, "If you will listen carefully to the voice of YHVH your Elohim, and do what is right in His sight, and listen to His commandments, and keep all His statutes, I will put none of the diseases on you which I have put on the Egyptians; for I, YHVH, am your healer."

Exodus 15:26

Trust this promise and do not give in to fear of disease. F.E.A.R (False Evidence Appearing Real) has killed more people than any virus. People compromise because of fear.

Sometimes He used a "fig poultice" or "mud on the eyes", sometimes He used His spit. He raised Talitha Kumi from the dead and then instructed them to feed her. So even Yeshua used supernatural and natural. Do not worship the natural supplementation, just use it as the Holy Spirit leads or your healthcare provider would advise.

Every three months most of the cells in your body regenerate but internal organs take about one year. Feed those cells with optimal nutrition!

And this is what I proclaim and pray through for my immune system:

Of David. Bless YHVH, O my soul, and all that is within me, bless His holy Name. Bless YHVH, O my soul, and forget not all His benefits: He forgives all your iniquity. He heals all your diseases.

Psalm 103-1-3

He said, "If you diligently listen to the voice of Adonai your God, do what is right in His eyes, pay attention to His mitzvot, and keep all His decrees, I will put none of the diseases on you which I have put on the Egyptians. For I am Adonai who heals you." Then they came to Elim, where there were twelve springs of water and seventy palm trees. So they camped there by the waters.

Exodus 15:26-27

But He was pierced because of our transgressions, crushed because of our iniquities. The chastisement for our shalom was upon Him, and by His stripes we are healed. We all like sheep have gone astray. Each of us turned to his own way. So Adonai has laid on Him the iniquity of us all. He was oppressed and He was afflicted yet He did not open His mouth. Like a lamb led to the slaughter, like a sheep before its shearers is silent, so He did not open His mouth.

Isaiah 53:5-7

He sent His word and healed them, and rescued them from their pits.

Psalm 107:20

Loved ones, I pray that all may go well with you and that you may be in good health, just as it is well with your soul.

3 John 2

The thief comes only to steal, slaughter, and destroy. I have come that they might have life, and have it abundantly!

John 10:10

Behold, I have given you authority to trample upon serpents and scorpions, and over all the power of the enemy; nothing will harm you.

Luke 10:19

Use His Word promises as Word prayers for your protection and health.

Death and life are in the power of the tongue, and those who love it will eat its fruit.

Proverbs 18:21 NASB

In closing, remember that Yah loves you and wants you well!

In His love to you,
Archbishop Dominiquae Bierman

Beloved, I pray that in all respects you may prosper and be in good health, just as your soul prospers.

3 John 1:2 NASB

Two Weddings & One Divorce

The First Marriage

The following illustration will explain why Christianity was 'the womb' of the Spanish Inquisition, the Crusades, and the Nazi Holocaust. Yahveh-God is looking to the church for repentance in order to influence the nations and fulfill the mandate of Matthew 28:19 *"Go and make disciples of all nations."*

The first and original church was married to a Jewish Husband by the name of Yeshua the Messiah and into His family the Jewish people (Ephesians 2:14 and Romans 11). The wedding ceremony took place in Jerusalem. It was ratified and sealed by the spilling of the blood of the Husband and by the breaking of His body. (Luke22:15–20) The time of this marriage was the holy biblical Feast of Passover. The fruit of this miraculous wedding was thousands and thousands of people, both Jews and Gentiles, saved and healed. Even the shadow of this holy bride healed the sick, as signs and wonders and miracles followed her wherever she went in the name of her Husband Yeshua.

This marriage led the wife to much suffering. Many in

the world did not love her Husband and tried to kill her by persecuting her and even throwing her to the lions during the Roman Empire's reign of terror. Those were hard years. After many years of suffering, Yeshua's wife had become weary. He had gone to prepare a place for her and had not come back yet.

She started to get tired from her lifestyle as an outcast, persecuted and hunted at every corner. She longed for peace at any price. She longed for the warm embrace of a Husband who would provide her with peace and security here on this earth. At her weakest point, an earthly king appeared. (Matthew 10:34, John 14:27, Jeremiah 8:11)

This earthly king was influential and powerful by earthly standards. He could stop the killing and persecution against her. He could give her the security she longed for *If* only she would agree to divorce this Jewish Husband of hers and completely separate from His family Israel, and from that Book that she treasured so much – where He had left her all of His instructions and the family legacy of God's Word.

This powerful king seemed to be a spiritual man. He claimed that her Jewish Husband had appeared to him in a dream and had given him the crown of the Roman Empire. His deceptive charm and appeasing manners managed to attract the very weary bride of Messiah, but not all were deceived. There was a portion of the bride/church/ecclesia that was not fooled by the charms of this deceitful king. These were the Messianic Jews of the time.

They were too rooted in the writings of the Holy Book and the ancient Hebrew Scriptures to be deceived. But the vast majority of the believers at that time were Gentiles, and they did not want any more suffering on behalf of the Book, its Author, or His family.

They wanted freedom and peace at all costs.

The powerful Constantine sang the song of peace and safety and prepared a bed of roses. The Gentile portion of the church slept with him, falling into violent adultery, and wounding the heart of her heavenly Jewish Husband. To appease the conscience of this adulterous church, Constantine decided to legalize this unholy union in the year AD 325 by means of a wedding ceremony called the Council of Nicaea and drew up an ungodly and illegal marriage contract called the Nicaean Creed.

He used his worldly power to draw all the gentile church fathers, which for the most part were already antisemitic and hated their Jewish roots. These church fathers were to be witnesses of this horrendous divorce and the adulterous new marriage between the predominantly Gentile church and another Jesus, a product of Constantine's own creation.

This alternative Savior came with another family, another book (totally disconnected from the ancient Hebrew writings), other customs, laws, festivals, traditions and ways of measuring time.

Knowing that his brand-new wife was accustomed to worshipping God, he organized for her a god that would suit her perfectly by not demanding any holiness from her. He presented a god of peace that was lenient towards a mixture of paganism and holiness: an all-inclusive god, who accepted all traditions and blended them into one.

Now Passover and First Fruits, the festival of Yeshua's resurrection, would become The Feast of Ishtar, the goddess of fertility, or Easter with bunny rabbits and Easter eggs. (At that time eggs were dipped in the blood of the babies sacrificed to the goddess, thus the tradition of painting the eggs.)

Now the day of worship would change from Shabbat to Sunday to eternalize the sun god who for now would be called Jesus – yet it was another Jesus and certainly not Yeshua, the Jewish Messiah.

Then the day of the winter solstice of witchcraft, called Saturnalia or Paganalia, celebrated on the 25th of December in the Roman Empire, was to acquire the name Christmas and would celebrate the birth of this false Messiah. The true Messiah was born during the holy biblical Feast of Tabernacles and followed the Hebrew biblical calendar, not the Roman one. (Daniel 7:25–27, Jeremiah 10:2–4 about the Christmas tree.)

The ancient Holy Book of the Hebrew Scriptures was to become obsolete, and its Laws done away with. Instead, Constantine compiled the apostolic writings, the letters of Paul and others into a new holy book and called it the New Testament. He gave this holy book his own perverse interpretation, completely divorced from the foundational Hebrew writings which he and his followers called the 'Old Testament.' (Matthew 5:17–21)

> "In rejecting their custom, we may transmit to our descendants the legitimate way of celebrating Easter... We ought not therefore to have anything in common with the Jew, for the Savior has shown us another way; our worship following a more legitimate and more convenient course (the order of the days of the week);

And consequently, in unanimously adopting this mode, we desire dearest brethren to separate ourselves from the detestable company of the Jew." (Excerpt from *The Nicene Creed*, year 325, found in *Eusebius, Vita Const. Lib III 18-20)*

Most Christians still follow this creed and its instructions today with the celebration of Easter, Christmas, Sunday (replacing Shabbat), and the rejection of the Laws of God.

Indeed, a new religion had been born. It had a gentile god by the name of Jesus Christ, an apostle by the name of Constantine, a new book by the name of the New Testament (although compiled from the apostolic writings, which are completely Yah-inspired, it was deceitfully interpreted through gentile eyes and gentile theologians), new traditions, and unholy festivals such as Easter, Christmas, Sunday, and Halloween.

And most importantly, *no Jews,* no, not even the Messiah. What has been the fruit of this adulterous marriage?

Either make the tree good and its fruit good, or else make the tree bad and its fruit bad; for a tree is known by its fruit.

Matthew 12:33

The fruits of the first holy matrimony were salvations and healings. The fruit of this ungodly and pagan marriage were forced conversions and killings, yes, even mass destructions of the family of Yeshua the Messiah (the true Husband), in the name of the false Jesus Christ god created by Constantine, a god who, according to Constantine in the Nicene Creed, had shown us *another way*. What was that way? It was a way of jealousy, hatred, killing, destruction, and lawlessness. Horrendous Christian events such as pogroms, the holy inquisition, and the holocaust, have taken place since this ungodly 4th century marriage and the creation of this false religion.

The hatred conveyed in the Nicene Creed against the Jews and anything Jewish, including the Torah and the Old Testament, has continued through the great Protestant Reformation of the 16th century, and it still influences Christians today.

The following excerpt is from *Our Hands are Stained with Blood* by Michael Brown, as he quotes directly from Martin Luther's writings.

Luther wrote this after he was frustrated from trying to evangelize the Jews and when he was old and sick:

"What shall we Christians do with this damned rejected race of Jews? First, their synagogues should be set on fire. Secondly, their homes should likewise be broken down and destroyed. Thirdly, they should be deprived of their prayer books and Talmud's. Fourthly, their rabbis must be forbidden under threat of death to teach anymore. Fifthly, passports and traveling privileges should be absolutely forbidden to the Jews... To sum up dear princes and nobles, who have Jews in your domains, if this advice of mine does not suit you, then find a better one. So that you and we may all be free of this insufferable, devilish burden – the Jews." (Luther and Brown)

Hitler followed Luther's instructions meticulously and quoted him while doing so. The fruit? Over six million Jews exterminated in horrendous death camps and gas chambers, and many of the survivors were scarred for life.

PROPHETIC ALTAR CALL

> After two days He will revive us; on the third day He will raise us up, that we may live in His sight. Let us know; let us pursue the knowledge of Yahveh. His going forth is established as the morning; He will come to us like the rain, like the latter and former rain to the earth.
>
> Hosea 6:2–3

The third day is upon us, the third millennium, and this is the Father's call to His third day church:

Come, let us return to Yeshua, to our Jewish Messiah, His Jewish family and His ancient Hebrew Scriptures. Come, let us reinterpret the New Testament through the eyes of the holy Scriptures. Let us separate ourselves from our pagan husband, Constantine, and his false Jesus and let us go back to the true Messiah Yeshua, to His Father's laws and precepts, to true divine holy grace, to true love and holiness. Let us return to Jerusalem and let us be made whole from centuries of adultery and paganism as we go back to the original apostolic Jewish roots of our faith.

In Yeshua's love and brokenness;
Archbishop Dr. Dominiquae & Rabbi Baruch Bierman

Disclaimer: *What this Article is Not Saying*

- It is *not* saying to go back to the laws of Rabbinic Judaism.
- It is *not* implying that all Christians have antisemitism.
- It is *not* disqualifying the countless believers who call on the name of Jesus Christ, meaning the *true* Jewish Messiah Yeshua.
- It is *not* disqualifying worship on Sunday, Monday, Tuesday, or any other day.
- It is *not* disqualifying the New Testament as Bible (Only the wrong, 'divorced' interpretations of it).

Revocation of the Council of Nicaea

From the letter of the Emperor (Constantine) to all those not present at the council. (Found in Eusebius, Vita Const., Lib III 18-20)

When the question relative to the sacred festival of Easter arose, it was universally thought that it would be convenient that all should keep the feast on one day; for what could be more beautiful and more desirable than to see this festival, through which we receive the hope of immortality, celebrated by all with one accord and in the same manner? It was declared to be particularly unworthy for this, the holiest of festivals, to follow the customs (the calculation) of the Jews who had soiled their hands with the most fearful of crimes, and whose minds were blinded. In rejecting their custom, we may transmit to our descendants the legitimate mode of celebrating Easter; which we have observed from the time of the Saviour's passion (according to the day of the week).

We ought not, therefore, to have anything in common with the Jew, for the Saviour has shown us another way; our worship following a more legitimate and more convenient course (the order of the days of the week: And consequently, in unanimously adopting this mode, we desire, dearest brethren to separate ourselves from the detestable company of the Jew. For it is truly shameful for us to hear them boast that without their direction, we could not keep this feast. How can they be in the right, they who, after the death of the Saviour, have no longer been led by reason but by wild violence, as their delusion may urge them? They do not possess the truth in this Easter question, for in their blindness and repugnance to all improvements they frequently celebrate two Passovers in the same year. We could not imitate those who are openly in error.

How, then, could we follow these Jews who are most certainly blinded by error? For to celebrate a Passover twice in one year, is totally inadmissible.

But even if this were not so it would still be your duty not to tarnish your soul by communication with such wicked people (the Jews). You should consider not only that the number of churches in these provinces make a majority, but also that it is right to demand what our reason approves, and that we should have nothing in

common with the Jews. (Gleaned from Dr. Henry R.
Percival's *"The Nicaean and Post Nicaean Fathers."* Vol.
XIV Grand Rapid: Erdmans pub. 1979, pgs. 54-55)

EXPOSING THE 23 LIES & DOCTRINAL ERRORS

1. 1. "When the question relative to the sacred festival of
   Easter..."
   The truth: sacred to pagan traditions, this is a pagan name
   derived from the goddess Ishtar. (Exodus 20:3, Hosea 2:17)

2. "...arose, it was universally..."
   The truth: Everyone in the universe? Is Constantine the
   king of the universe? (Isaiah 14:3)

3. "...thought that it would be convenient..."
   The truth: God does not call us to convenience but obedience. (John 15:10)

4. "...that all should keep the feast on one day; for what could
   be more beautiful and more desirable than to see this
   festival, through which we receive the hope of immortality,
   celebrated by all with one accord and in the same manner?"
   The truth: Without Jews? John 17:21, unity between Jew
   and Gentile brings the salvation of all mankind. (Psalms 133
   and Isaiah 56)

5. "...It was declared to be particularly unworthy..."
   The truth: Yahveh's choice of dates is "unworthy" to Con-

stantine as he sets himself above God's choosing of timings. (Daniel 7:25 and Isaiah 14:13 [Lucifer])

6. "...for this, the holiest of festivals to follow the customs (the calculation) of the Jews..."

The truth: Which are the original and true calculations? (Leviticus 23:1, Jeremiah 31:31–34)

7. "...who had soiled their hands with the most fearful of crimes, and whose minds were blinded..."

The truth: In John 10:17–18, Yeshua lays His own life down (See also John 3:16). The accusation that "The Jews killed Christ" has been the incentive for the extermination of millions of Jews from that point onwards and until this day, including the Holocaust. (See Matthew 7:17–20, the fruit of this theology)

8. "...In rejecting their custom..."

The truth: God's custom is according to His Word.

9. "...we may transmit to our descendants the legitimate..."

The truth: "Legitimate" according to Constantine, but not according to the Word of God. (Matthew 26:2, Leviticus 23:1–4, Genesis 1:14, John 20:1–9, Matthew 12:39)

10. "...mode of celebrating Easter which we have observed..."

The truth: This pagan name and feast are not mentioned in the Holy Scriptures.[21]

11. "We ought not therefore to have anything in common

---

[21]   Easter is the name of the goddess of fertility, Ishtar. This pagan feast morphed into a Christian celebration replacing the Biblical Passover and the feasts of First fruits and Unleavened Bread.

with the Jew, for the Savior has shown us another way."

The truth: Yeshua is Jewish, so if nothing is in common with the Jews, nothing is in common with the Messiah. (Matthew 1, John 19:19, Luke 1:59, Luke 2:21)

12. "our worship following a more legitimate and more convenient course, the order of the days of the week"

The truth: Constantine legitimizes his own ideas in order to gain political power and control, and he attempts to dethrone the Word of God on this subject, setting himself and his opinions above Yah and His unchanging Word.

13. "...And consequently in unanimously..."

The truth: without the Jews from which salvation comes! (John 4:22)

14. "...adopting this mode, we desire, dearest brethren to separate ourselves from the detestable company of the Jew for it is truly shameful for us to hear them boast that without their direction we could not keep this feast. How can they be in the right, they who, after the death of the Savior..."

The truth: Romans 11:15–20 warns the Gentiles not to be arrogant against the Jews or Gentiles will be cut of the Olive tree!

15. "...have no longer been led by reason..."

The truth: True sons of God are not led by reason or Greek philosophy but by the Spirit of God. Since Constantine and the Council of Nicaea, the church in its vast majority has been led by reason and by theologians instead of by powerful apostles. (Romans 8:14, Ephesians 2:20) - These are all Jewish.

16. "But by wild violence, as their delusion may urge them"

The truth: What wild violence is he talking about? Unsupported accusations were used many times to incite the masses against the Jews, like in the Protocols of the Elders of Zion.[22]

17. "They do not possess the truth in this Easter question, for in their blindness and [15th lie] repugnance to all improvements."

The truth: Traditions of demons and men make null and void the Word of God (Matthew 15:3, 4; Mark 7:13)

18. "They frequently celebrate two Passovers in the same year. We could not imitate those who are openly in error. How, then, could we follow these Jews who are most certainly blinded by error?"

The truth: Is following the biblical customs error? Who is really blinded here? Gentiles are supposed to be grafted into Israel's Olive tree and not vice versa! (Romans 11:15–20)

19. "For to celebrate a Passover twice in one year is totally inadmissible."

The truth: It is totally scriptural. (2 Chronicles 30:1–3)

20. "But even if this were not so it would still be your duty not to tarnish your soul by communication with such wicked people (the Jews)."

The truth: In other words, Constantine's purpose is to sep-

---

[22]   The *Protocols of the Elders of Zion* is the most notorious and widely distributed antisemitic publication of modern times. (https://encyclopedia. ushmm.org/content/en/article/protocols-of-the-elders-of-zion)

arate from the Jews and the Torah, no matter what! Why? 1 John 4:1–3 states that the spirit of anti-Messiah (in operation through Constantine) removes the identity of Messiah as a Jew, and sets himself above God, His Word, and His sovereign choice of choosing the Jews to bring salvation.

21. "You should consider not only that the number of churches in these provinces make a majority"

The truth: God has never worked with "majorities", but with obedience. Trusting in the arm of the flesh or the opinions of men brings about a curse! (Deuteronomy 28:1–14, Jeremiah 17:5, Judges 7:2–8; 1 Samuel 14:6)

22. "...but also that it is right to demand what our reason approves..."

The truth: Human reasoning? (1 Corinthians 1:27, Isaiah 29:14b)

23. "...and that we should have nothing in common with the Jews."

The truth: Jews include the Jewish Messiah and His salvation. (John 4:22, Romans 11:15–20) He set the Gentile part of the church onto a path of self-destruction, remaining a wild olive tree instead of being grafted into the cultivated Olive tree – which is Israel – because of arrogance, thereby removing the foundations of the Jewish apostles and prophets. (Psalms 11:3, Ephesians 2:20, Revelation 21:14)

Prayer Renouncing the First Council of Nicaea

Please pray. You can copy and pass it on, and please let us know of your decision.

Before the Almighty God of Israel, I stand and hereby renounce the First Council of Nicaea as led by Constantine. I renounce its foundation and all the anti-Jewish fruit that came out of it. I renounce every doctrinal error and every lie in it, including replacement theology in all of its aspects.

I hereby affirm my faith in Yahveh, the God of Israel, who is the Creator of the Universe and my Father through the atoning death of His Holy Son Yeshua, who is both the promised Jewish Messiah and the Son of God who became a human. I hereby affirm my faith in the resurrection of Yeshua the Messiah and the outpouring of the Holy Spirit of God from the Day of Shavuot (Pentecost) and onwards, to all that repent and believe in the Son. I hereby affirm my belief that I am grafted into the Olive Tree that represents Israel, and together with the believing Jewish people, I will inherit eternal life. I hereby affirm that the God of Israel will never forsake His people, neither will

He forget His covenant with the Jews or with the Ecclesia (Called out Ones - Church).

I thank You, Holy Father, for removing all the curses that have come into my life and into my nation due to our belief in the tenets of faith stated in the Council of Nicaea concerning the Jews and the Jewish foundations of the faith. I beg You and thank You for pouring out Your great mercy and forgiveness over myself, my family, and my nation. I hereby commit myself to walk in truth as You reveal it to me and in love with all my fellow men and especially my (and the Church's) spiritual parents, the Jewish people, according to Genesis 12:1-3.

Connect With Us

Visit our websites & follow us on social media

United Nations for Israel

Take a stand for the restoration of Israel and transform your nation into a sheep nation, one person at a time. Become a member and join our monthly members' online conferences to get equipped!

www.UnitedNationsForIsrael.org
info@unitednationsforisrael.org

Israel Tours

Travel through Israel with our "Bible Schools on Wheels" and watch the Hebrew Holy Scriptures come alive.
www.zionsgospel.com/tours-and-events/

Global Revival MAP (GRM) Israeli Bible Institute

Take the most comprehensive video Bible school online
that focuses on the restoration of all things.
www.GRMBibleInstitute.com
info@grmbibleinstitute.com

Global Re-Education Initiative
(GRI) Against Anti-Semitism

Discover the Jewish Messiah and defeat religious anti-Semitism!
Order *The Identity Theft* and GRI Online Course Package
www.Against-Antisemitism.com
info@against-antisemitism.com

From Israel to the Nations TV Programs

Watch Archbishop Dominiquae Bierman's TV programs
taped in the land of Israel!
Roku Channel: **Israel Revival**
YouTube: **Dominiquae Bierman TV**
www.youtube.com/@DominiquaeBiermanTV
Broadcasting Schedule: www.zionsgospel.com/tv/

MAP Prison Ministry

Through our prison ministry, pioneered by Rabbi Baruch
Bierman, GRM Bible School is studied in prisons all over the USA.
For more information & to support:
www.zionsgospel.com/map-prison-ministry/

Sign our petition to ban neo-Nazi ideology in America and share it forward!

www.change.org/BanNeoNazism-Evil-Can-Be-Stopped

For more information about the founder of the ministries:
www.DominiquaeBierman.com

Books & Music

For more books by Dr. Dominiquae Bierman,
order online: **www.ZionsGospel.com**

The Voice of These Ashes
What are the Ashes of the Exterminated Jewish People Crying For?

The Identity Theft
The Return of the 1st Century Messiah

"Yes!"
The Dramatic Life Story of an Israeli Woman who Falls and Rises
Again Because of one Word: "YES!"

Restoring the Glory – Volume I: The Original Way
The Ancient Paths Rediscovered

The MAP Revolution (free E-book)
Exposing Theologies that Obstruct the Bride

Eradicating the Cancer of Religion
Hint: All People Have It!

The Healing Power of the Roots
It's a Matter of Life and Death!

Grafted In
It's Time to Return to Greatness!

Sheep Nations
It's Time to Take the Nations!

Yeshua is the Name
The Important Restoration of the True Name of the Messiah!

The Key of Abraham
The Blessing or the Curse?

Stormy Weather
Judgment Has Begun and Revival is Knocking at the Doors!

Restoration of Holy Giving
Releasing the True 1,000-Fold Blessing

The Bible Cure for Africa and the Nations
The Key to the Restoration of all Africa

Vision Negev
The Awesome Restoration of the Sephardic Jews!

Defeating Depression
This Book is a Kiss from Heaven!

From Sickology to a Healthy Logic
The Product of 18 Years Walking Through Psychiatric Hospitals

Addicts Turning to God
The Biblical Way to Handle Addicts & Addictions

The Woman Factor: Freedom from Womanophobia
by Rabbi Baruch Bierman with Dominiquae Bierman

The Spider That Survived Hurricane Irma (free E-book)
God's Call for America to Repent

The Revival of the Third Day (free E-book)
The Return to Yeshua the Jewish Messiah

Tribute to the Jew in You Music Book
Notes for the Tribute to the Jew in You Music Album

Music Albums
Abba Shebashamayim

Uru

Retorno

The Key of Abraham

Tribute to the Jew in You

Tribute to the Jew in You Instrumental

Support the Mission

Contact Us

Archbishop Dr. Dominiquae & Rabbi Baruch Bierman

www.ZionsGospel.com | shalom@zionsgospel.com

Kad-Esh MAP Ministries

www.kad-esh.org | info@kad-esh.org

United Nations for Israel

www.unitednationsforisrael.org

info@unitednationsforisrael.org

52 Tuscan Way, Ste 202-412, St. Augustine,

Florida 32092, USA

+1-972-301-7087

www.ingramcontent.com/pod-product-compliance
Lightning Source LLC
Chambersburg PA
CBHW021651120626
46545CB00002B/806